Amazing Space

Written by Sophie Allan and Josh Barker
Illustrated by Tim Smart

Editors John Hort, Robin Moul, Lizzie Munsey
US Editor Margaret Parrish
US Senior Editor Shannon Beatty
Designers Charlotte Jennings, Roohi Rais,
Mansi Dwivedi, Karen Hood, Samantha Richiardi
Jacket Designer Charlotte Jennings
Senior Picture Researcher Sakshi Saluja
DTP designer Dheeraj Singh
Managing Editor Penny Smith
Managing Art Editor Ivy Sengupta
Production Editor Becky Fallowfield
Production Controller Ben Radley
Delhi Creative Head Malavika Talukder
Deputy Art Director Mabel Chan
Managing Director Sarah Larter

First American Edition, 2024
Published in the United States by DK Publishing,
a division of Penguin Random House LLC
1745 Broadway, 20th Floor, New York, NY 10019

Copyright © 2024 Dorling Kindersley Limited
24 25 26 27 28 10 9 8 7 6 5 4 3 2 1
001–340527–Aug/2024

A catalog record for this book
is available from the Library of Congress.
ISBN 978-0-7440-9846-4

DK books are available at special discounts when purchased
in bulk for sales promotions, premiums, fund-raising,
or educational use.
For details, contact: DK Publishing Special Markets,
1745 Broadway, 20th Floor, New York, NY 10019
SpecialSales@dk.com

Printed and bound in China

www.dk.com

This book was made with Forest
Stewardship Council™ certified
paper – one small step in DK's
commitment to a sustainable future.
Learn more at **www.dk.com/uk/**
information/sustainability

Over the course of writing this book, we have been able to cover many corners of space. The wide range of topics found in space is what makes it so interesting. If you like robots and technology, you can explore the awesome telescopes or rockets we build. If you're interested in humans and biology, you can follow the inspiring journey of astronauts. If the weird and unusual excites you, dive headfirst into black holes and supernova.

We believe that whatever you're interested in, you can find amazing examples of that out in space. So, as you explore this book, we hope you find some things that fascinate you and encourage you to ask questions, as we unravel the mysteries of the universe together.

Sophie Allan & Josh Barker

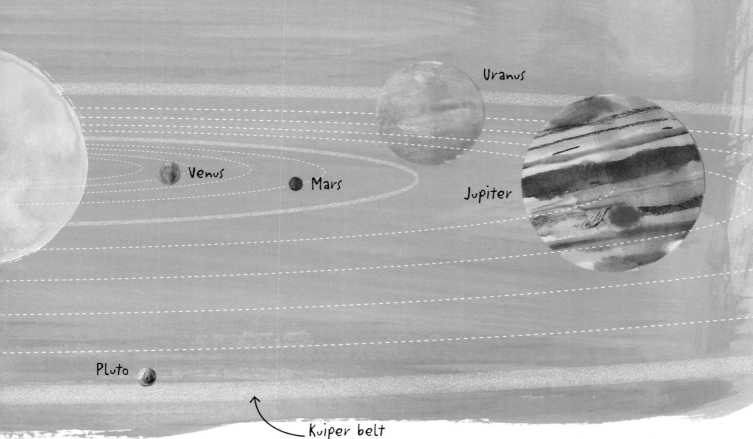

Uranus

Venus

Mars

Jupiter

Pluto

Kuiper belt

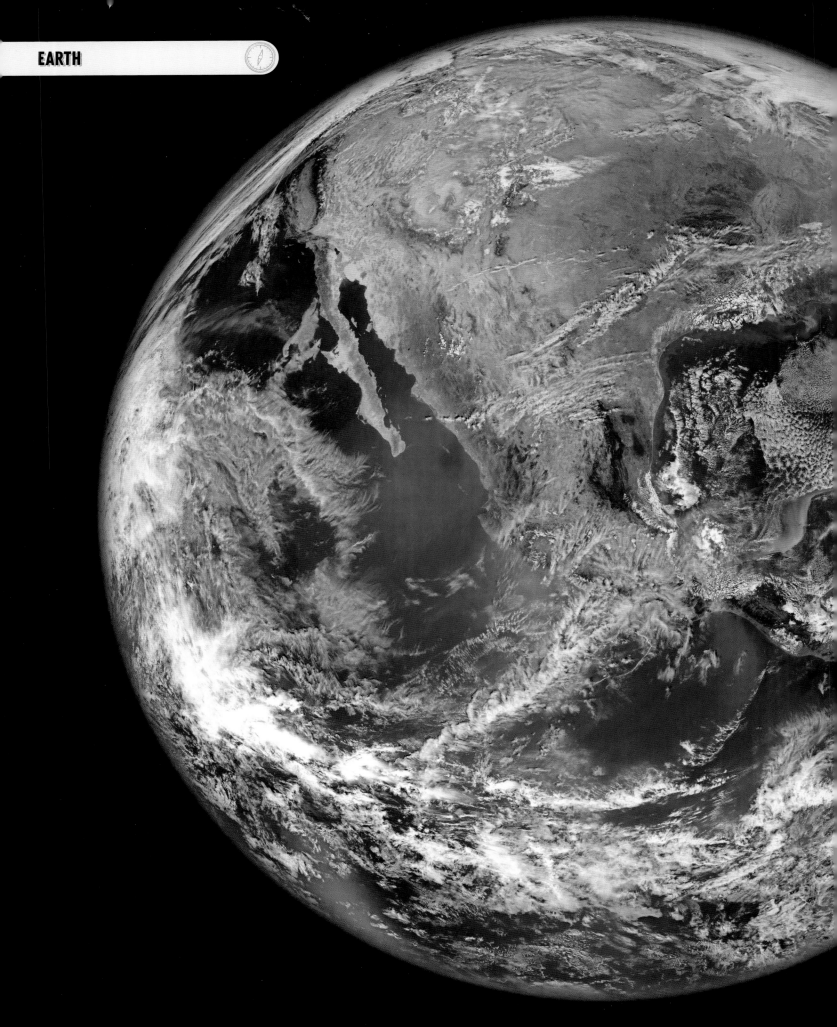

CONTENTS

INTRODUCTION

Space is a truly incredible place; it is vast and mysterious and contains some of the most beautiful and interesting objects ever found. We, like many of our human ancestors, find it fascinating, and we hope you do too.

Space has always inspired humans to ask the big questions. We looked to the sky and wondered what was out there. What are those twinkling lights? Could we ever go to the moon? Where do we fit in the cosmos?

As we created better tools for peering into space, we discovered amazing things. We've spotted the birth and death of stars, tracked asteroids and comets whizzing around our solar system, and even sent humans out to walk on the surface of the moon.

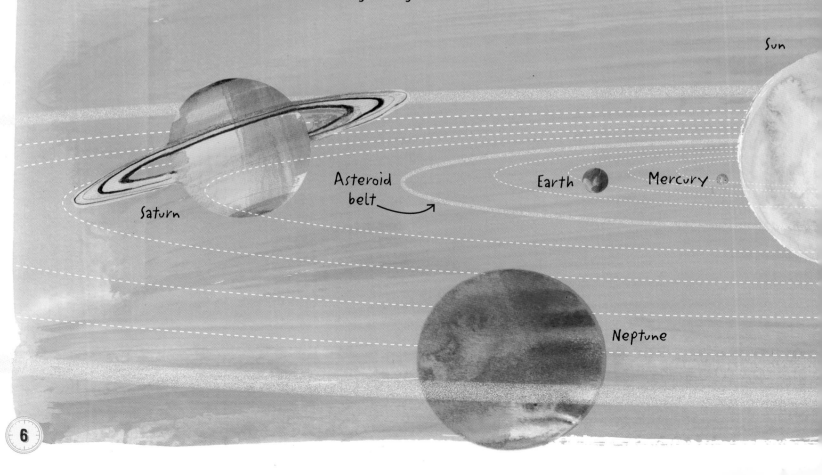

Sun

Saturn

Asteroid belt

Earth

Mercury

Neptune

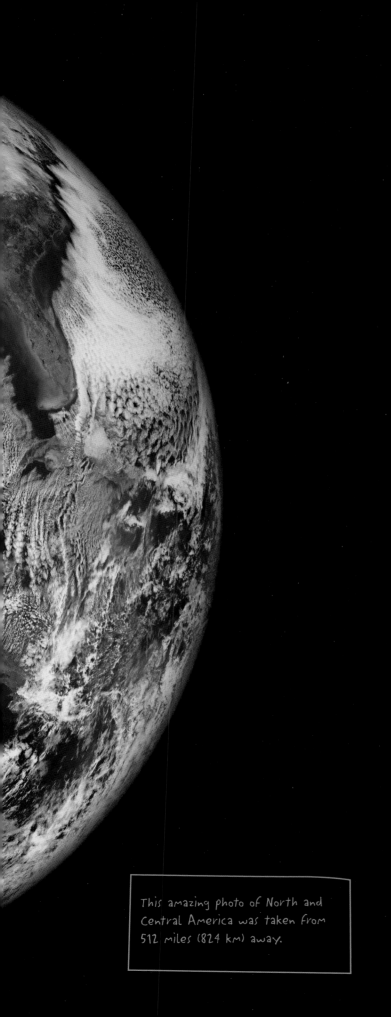

This amazing photo of North and Central America was taken from 512 miles (824 km) away.

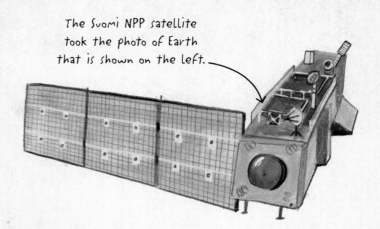

The Suomi NPP satellite took the photo of Earth that is shown on the left.

EARTH FROM SPACE

Earth is covered with amazing sights. People travel the world to photograph oceans, forests, mountains, cities, and more. But to really appreciate these wonders, and to truly understand our incredible planet, the best views are from space.

At night, astronauts looking down from satellites can use the bright lights of cities and towns to figure out which country they are looking at.

NEW PERSPECTIVES

High above the surface of Earth, human-made machines called satellites travel around our planet. They follow roughly circular paths, called orbits. From up above, satellites get a spectacular view of our world. Some of them take detailed pictures that help us understand our planet.

Satellites orbiting Earth

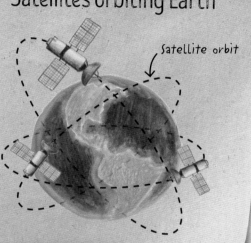

Satellite orbit

Speedy orbits

There are thousands of satellites currently orbiting Earth. They have a variety of uses, including weather forecasting, communications, and navigation.

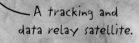

A tracking and data relay satellite.

Earthrise

Not all images of the Earth are taken from satellites. On December 24, 1968, American astronaut William Anders took the famous photograph *Earthrise* while orbiting the moon.

Sculpted Earth

Weather is a powerful force of nature and can cause massive destruction. It can also craft beautiful shapes in rock and sand. Satellites can give us a new perspective on the weathering of our planet.

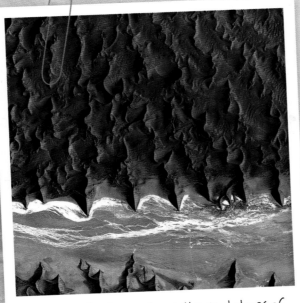

This satellite image shows the sand dunes of the Namib Desert in Namibia.

Natural wonder

Australia's Great Barrier Reef is home to 400 types of coral—fragile sea creatures that form beautiful underwater forests called reefs. Satellite images can capture the scale and health of the reef.

This photograph shows 10 miles (16 km) of the 1,700-mile (2,300-km) reef.

Thousands of species of sea creatures live in the Great Barrier Reef.

An aurora lights up the sky above Norway.

Auroras occur around Earth's North and South poles.

North Pole

South Pole

AURORAS

When conditions are perfect, a spectacular natural light-show surrounds both ends of Earth. These eerie bands of dancing, green-and-red light are called auroras. They have captured people's imaginations for centuries. Today, many people travel long distances to see this spectacular sight.

The Finnish word for an aurora is *revontulet*, which means "fox fire." This is because Finnish people once believed that auroras were caused by a giant fox swishing its tail across the sky.

THE BIGGEST LIGHT SHOW

The auroras are also known as the northern and southern lights, because the North and South poles are where the light show is brightest. The source of the lights was a mystery for a long time. We now know they are created by our active, unpredictable sun.

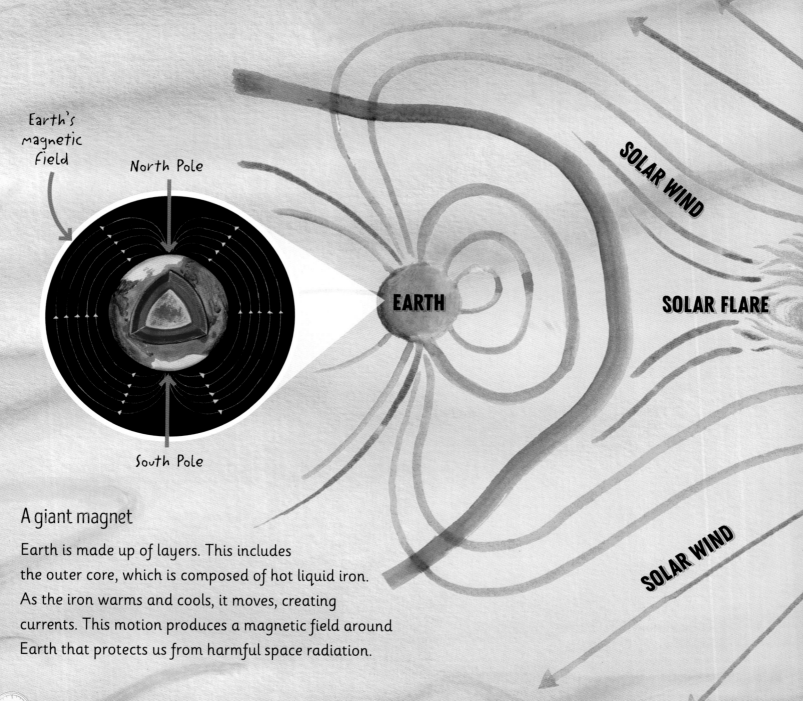

Earth's magnetic field

North Pole

South Pole

EARTH

SOLAR WIND

SOLAR FLARE

SOLAR WIND

A giant magnet

Earth is made up of layers. This includes the outer core, which is composed of hot liquid iron. As the iron warms and cools, it moves, creating currents. This motion produces a magnetic field around Earth that protects us from harmful space radiation.

Our active sun

The sun is a giant ball of hot hydrogen and helium gases. It is constantly active, throwing out high-energy radiation into space. This radiation is called solar wind. Sometimes, huge solar flares fling even more radiation out into space.

SUN

Lighting up the skies

If Earth blocks solar flares, the radiation squashes our planet's magnetic field, causing it to temporarily snap. This lets some radiation filter down to Earth's poles. The radiation interacts with the gases in our atmosphere, making it glow.

Auroras glow green due to oxygen in the atmosphere.

Pesquet's photo shows an aurora stretching all the way around Earth.

Spectacular auroras

Auroras can be breathtaking. French astronaut Thomas Pesquet snapped this incredible image of the auroras from a window on the International Space Station.

Artemis 1 launched in November 2022 from the Kennedy Space Center in Florida.

The Artemis SLS rocket will play a key role in future NASA missions.

ROCKETS

Rockets are the only vehicles we currently have that can leave Earth and head out into space. So, to send objects into space, we have to use rockets. Scientists are continually working to improve the technology behind rockets—the ones in use today are very different from the simpler models that we started with.

This photo shows the first rocket to use liquid fuel—the same type of fuel used for all rockets today. Next to it is the rocket's inventor, American engineer Robert Goddard.

BLASTING OFF

Rocket technology is actually quite simple. A rocket engine pushes hot gas through it very quickly, which creates a force, causing the rocket to move. While the idea is simple, pushing enough gas through safely can be difficult.

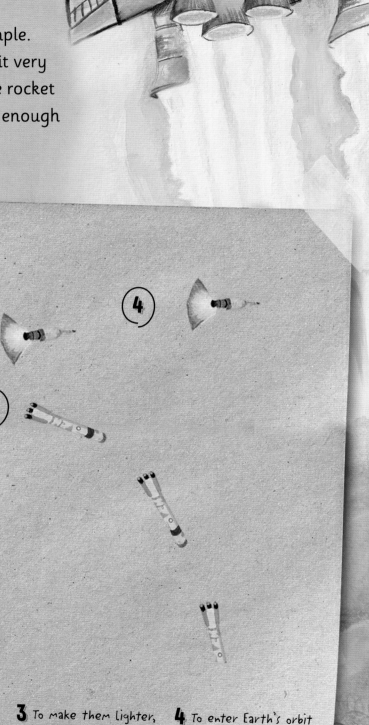

How rockets launch

There are several important stages involved when launching a rocket:

1 The rocket must produce greater thrust than its own weight to allow it to push off from the ground.

2 To leave the atmosphere, a rocket needs to travel at around 7 miles/sec (11 km/sec).

3 To make them lighter, rockets often drop sections during takeoff. This is so fuel isn't wasted.

4 To enter Earth's orbit using as little fuel as possible, rockets follow a curved path.

Early rockets

The first rockets were invented by Chinese scientists thousands of years ago. They were similar to fireworks and were driven by a fuel called gunpowder. These rockets were mainly used as weapons or at celebrations.

A man named Wan Hu apparently tried to get to space by attaching rockets to his chair!

REUSABLE ROCKETS

Returning home

Getting rockets back from space once they are launched is very difficult. The Space Shuttle was the first rocket designed to return to Earth safely, so that it could be used again.

Help at launch

Scientists are always working on new designs and technology for rockets. Virgin Galactic's SpaceShipTwo is carried by a special airplane. It then uses its own engines to get into space.

Modern rockets

By the 1950s, better designs and more powerful rocket fuels had made rocket engines powerful enough to reach space. The first human-made object to be sent into space was a satellite, Sputnik 1, in 1957.

Soyuz rockets have been launched almost 2,000 times, sending astronauts and satellites on many missions.

Safe landing

Some modern rockets are now fully reusable and are able to land on boats. Here, SpaceX Falcon 9 has landed on its recovery barge.

Vesta is in the asteroid belt.

FUTURE FUELS

Rocket technology hasn't changed much in hundreds of years. Newer rockets are bigger and more powerful than older ones, but they are all powered by flammable fuel and use fire to release the energy. To explore farther into space, scientists are now investigating new and exciting types of fuel, engines, and technology.

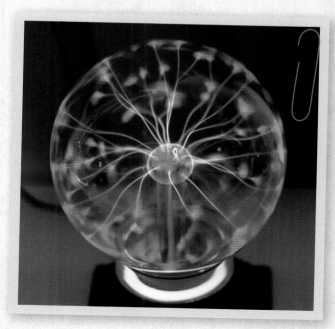

Ion engines are powered by xenon gas—the same gas that is often used in plasma lamps. It is safe and easy to store, unlike rocket fuel. Xenon thrusters can fire for many years.

This is an artist's impression of the Dawn spacecraft, using an ion engine to reach the asteroid Vesta.

NEW POWER

Rockets have been extremely successful for almost a century. However, rocket fuel is very heavy, meaning that more than 95 percent of every rocket launched is made up of just the fuel and engines. Developing new ways to power spacecraft will help us explore deeper into space.

Skylon is an idea for a "spaceplane"

SABRE engine

Rocket evolution

The first step in our quest for new rockets is to make existing rockets better. SABRE, a new type of engine, acts like an airplane engine until it reaches a high enough altitude, then it switches to rocket mode. This saves weight and space and allows the spacecraft SABRE is attached to be reusable.

Thrust chambers release hot gas

Compressor

Turbine

The SABRE engine takes lots of air and squashes it into a tiny area, while cooling it extremely quickly. The engine mixes the air with fuel and burns it.

Solar sails

The idea of attaching giant mirrors to spacecraft so that they work as engines is called solar sailing. In 2010, the Japanese space agency successfully used a solar sail to get a spacecraft to Venus, showing that we can use the sun's light to push us around the solar system.

Solar sails are tethered to the main body of a spacecraft.

Sailing on light

The sail has a large surface area to catch photons.

Sun

Photons (light particles from the sun) have energy and movement.

The photons reflect off the sail, pushing it along.

IKAROS small-scale solar-powered sail demonstration satellite

Warp drive

Some scientists think that we may be able to bend space to make it easier to travel. A small team of NASA scientists is investigating if this would be possible. They hope to make a "warp drive," which sounds like something out of a science fiction film!

Things with gravity "bend" the space around them.

23

The first spacewalk by a human not connected to a spacecraft was made by American astronaut Bruce McCandless in 1984.

Bruce McCandless began his spacewalk from the Space Shuttle Challenger.

HUMANS IN SPACE

Humans have long wanted to travel among the stars. Once we developed rockets and learned more about the universe, we were able to begin visiting space in person. However, space is a tricky place to survive, and some weird and wonderful things can happen to us there.

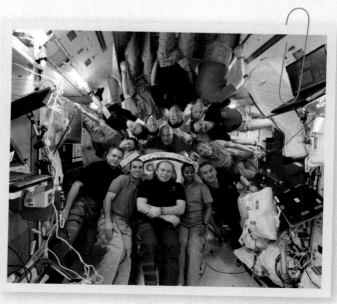

Humans in space often stay on spacecraft called space stations. In 2010, an amazing 13 people were all on board the largest one, the International Space Station, at once.

LIFE OFF EARTH

The weightless environment of space makes it a fantastic place to conduct science experiments. The human body, however, is not designed to work without gravity. We have to make many small changes so that life in space is comfortable for astronauts, and to ensure that they stay safe and healthy during their adventures.

To use a treadmill, astronauts must be strapped down, otherwise they would float away!

Staying strong

On Earth, we constantly battle gravity as we move around. Astronauts in space can float—they don't need big strong bones and muscles to move. To prevent their bodies from getting weaker in space, they must spend hours a day doing exercise.

EATING FRESH

Feeding astronauts is a vital part of keeping them in space for a long time. To keep food fresh, it is sealed in airtight packages. Mission control makes sure that astronauts have a healthy balanced diet. Currently, all food has to be taken into space, but astronauts are working on experiments to grow food out there.

Sandra Magnus preparing some lunch. Tortilla wraps are used because they make fewer crumbs than regular bread.

Waste disposal

Using the toilet is complicated for astronauts. The lack of gravity in space means waste doesn't fall, so toilets must use suction. Solid and liquid waste are separated: solids are disposed of, but liquid waste is recycled, purified, and turned back into drinking water.

A toilet on board the International Space Station.

Jasmin Moghbeli processes microbe samples.

A busy day

Astronauts work hard to make the most of their time in space. They usually work 16 hours a day for six-and-a-half days a week, doing experiments and looking after the space station. Most astronauts even take on extra work in their time off!

Sultan Al Neyadi undertakes a science experiment.

The dining table looks a little different in space. Food would float off plates, so it is served in its packaging.

Japanese astronaut Soichi Noguchi checking on the space radishes.

Edwin "Buzz" Aldrin walks on the surface of the moon in 1969.

The moon

EXTRAORDINARY ASTRONAUTS

Space is a difficult place for people to live and work. However, with the support of their Earth-based mission controllers, some astronauts have achieved incredible things. These brave explorers have helped push the boundaries of what we thought was possible in space exploration.

In 1961, Yuri Gagarin became the first person ever to travel into space.

THE STARS OF SPACE

More than 600 people have made the epic journey into space. They have carried out amazing scientific research, flown daring repair missions, and helped us to understand the universe. Here are just a few of the fantastic things that astronauts have achieved.

The crew of Apollo 13: Jim Lovell, Thomas Mattingly, and Fred Haise.

Distant travelers

The crew of Apollo 13 is well-known because the mission nearly ended in disaster, and the astronauts almost didn't make it home. They hold the record for traveling the farthest distance away from Earth—a whopping 250,000 miles (400,000 km)!

In 1970, part of the spacecraft used on the Apollo 13 mission exploded and the crew had to abort the mission. Everyone made it back to Earth safely, thanks to some very quick problem-solving from the crew.

APOLLO 13 MISSION SPACECRAFT

Valentina Tereshkova

VOSTOK 6

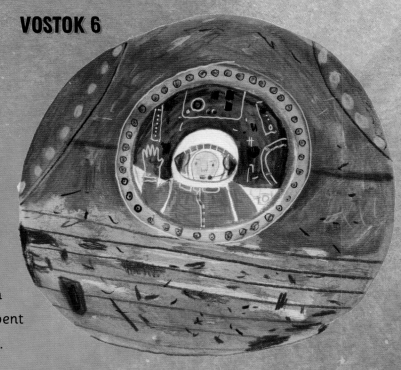

Flying solo

On June 16, 1963, Valentina Tereshkova flew into space. She was selected for the mission because of her skills as a parachutist, and she spent three days photographing the Earth from above. She was the first woman in space and still holds the records of youngest woman in space and only woman to complete a solo space flight.

Mae Jemison was a mission specialist on the Space Shuttle Endeavour in 1992. She was the first Black woman to visit space.

Brazilian Marcos Pontes visited the International Space Station in 2006. He was the first person to represent a southern-hemisphere country in space.

Global exploration

Exploring space is a task that unites countries from around the world. More than 45 nationalities have been represented in space and more than 20 have visited the International Space Station.

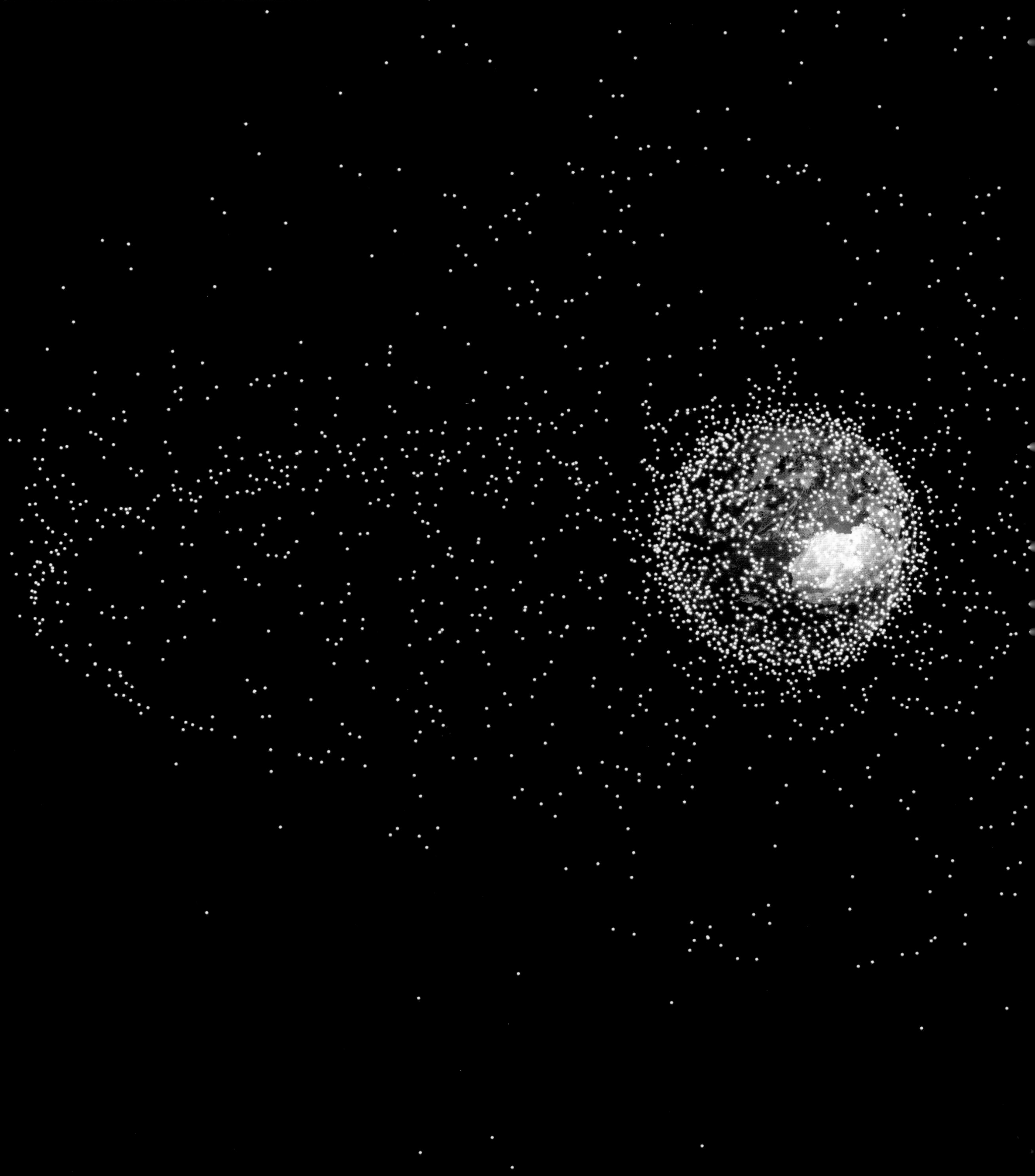

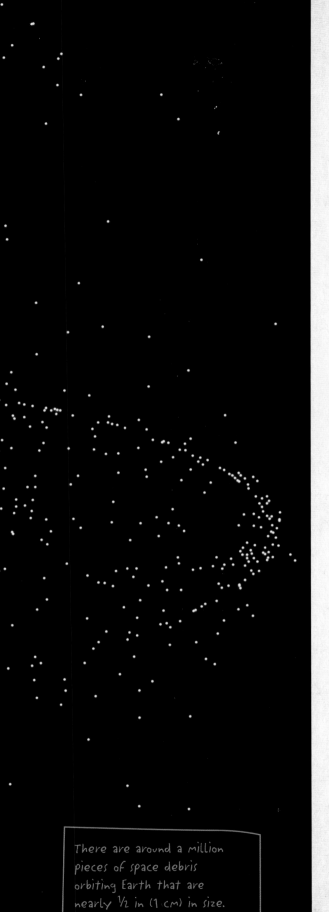

SPACE JUNK

Earth is surrounded by billions of pieces of space junk, from bits of dust and rock to the remains of space missions, including flecks of paint, frozen fuel, and damaged parts of satellites. The area of space around Earth is basically a graveyard for pieces of rockets and satellites.

Solar panels in space are often damaged by impacts with space objects. The most violent collisions are with meteorites.

There are around a million pieces of space debris orbiting Earth that are nearly ½ in (1 cm) in size.

LITTERING SPACE

Imagine sitting in your spacecraft when it is suddenly struck by a piece of space junk traveling at tens of thousands of miles per hour. This is a reality for astronauts, and it affects satellites, too. When traveling at high speed, even an object as small as a grain of sand has the same force on impact as a bullet.

Disused satellites are one of the larger types of space junk.

Kessler collision chaos

American scientist Donald J. Kessler realized that as more satellites were left in space, they were more likely to collide, creating more debris. This in turn would cause more collisions. In 2009, a US and Russian satellite collided with one another and their debris spread, proving Kessler right.

Russian satellite Kosmos-2251's orbit

Collision point

US satellite Iridium's orbit

The two satellites collided at the red point above.

Iridium's debris cloud

Kosmos-2251's debris cloud

Ten minutes after the collision, the debris cloud was small.

But after three hours, the cloud was bigger, spreading space junk far and wide.

The giant radar system at RAF Fylingdales detects and tracks orbiting objects.

Tracking junk

To keep our astronauts and satellites safe, the larger pieces of space junk are tracked by a network of telescopes and radar systems, such as the radar at RAF Fylingdales in the UK. We can now track pieces of debris as small as a pea!

We may be able to clean up space by using satellites to harpoon junk.

Clean space

Despite the huge amount of debris that exists, it is possible to clean up space. In 2019, the NanoRacks-Remove Debris satellite successfully demonstrated that a harpoon could be fired at, and hold onto, space debris.

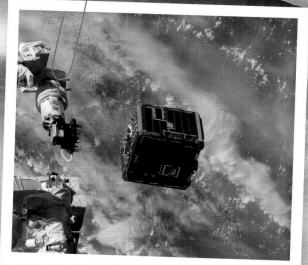

The NanoRacks-Remove Debris satellite was released from the International Space Station.

Laika was a stray dog from the former Soviet Union. She was the first animal to orbit the Earth successfully, on board Sputnik 2.

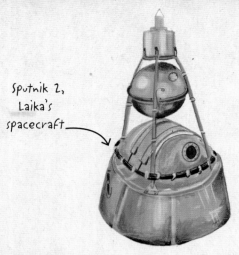

Sputnik 2, Laika's spacecraft

ANIMALS IN SPACE

Before humans could visit space, animals were sent to test whether it was possible for living things to survive. Since then, animals have continued to be sent into space so that scientists can investigate everything from future space farm-animals to medical research, which could benefit millions of humans on Earth.

Belka and Strelka were launched into space in 1960 and returned to Earth safely. Strelka went on to have puppies, and one of them was given to the president of the United States!

IT STARTED WITH FLIES

The first animals ever launched into space were fruit flies. More recently, animals have lived in specially designed habitats on space stations that allow them to adjust to living in orbit. Astronauts study how the animals perform and adapt to help us plan for future missions.

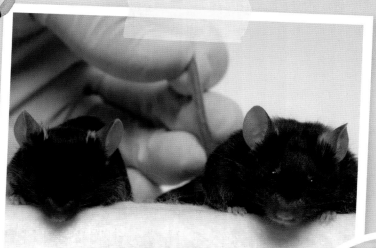

Mice in space

Mice have much shorter lives than humans. Because of this, we can see what happens to creatures when they spend a big chunk of their lives in space. Mice in space adapt well when they can exercise, showing us that astronauts need to be able to exercise in space.

The Rodent Habitation Module on the International Space Station allows rodents to climb all sides of their cages so that they can get around easily in zero gravity.

ANIMALS IN SPACE

Laika (1957)

The first animal to orbit Earth successfully, Laika, sadly, didn't make it back.

Belka and Stelka (1960)

These dogs traveled with 42 mice, a gray rabbit, two rats, flies, and plants and fungi.

Ham (1961)

Ham underwent two years of training before he became the first great ape in space.

Hector (1961)

Hector was a French rat who wore a personalized space suit during his successful flight.

Tough tardigrades

Tardigrades are tiny creatures that you need a microscope to see. They are one of the toughest creatures on Earth, able to survive in extreme conditions. A mission called Tardigrades In Space (TARDIS) also proved that they could survive for 10 days in space itself!

Japanese astronaut Akihiko Hoshide with tardigrades in zero gravity.

Certain zebra fish have largely see-through outsides, which allow us to see the skeleton, muscles, and organs inside.

Zebra fish

Floating in space is bad for your bones, as they lose calcium and then can easily break. A simple way to study bones is to use a creature with a visible skeleton, such as the zebra fish. Those on the ISS were specially adapted so that parts of them would glow under certain conditions!

Félicette (1963)

Félicette was a stray cat from Paris, France. She is the only cat to have left Earth.

Tortoises (1968)

Two unnamed Russian tortoises became the first animals to orbit the moon.

Arabella and Anita (1973)

While on board the Skylab 3 space station, these two spiders were the first to make a web in space.

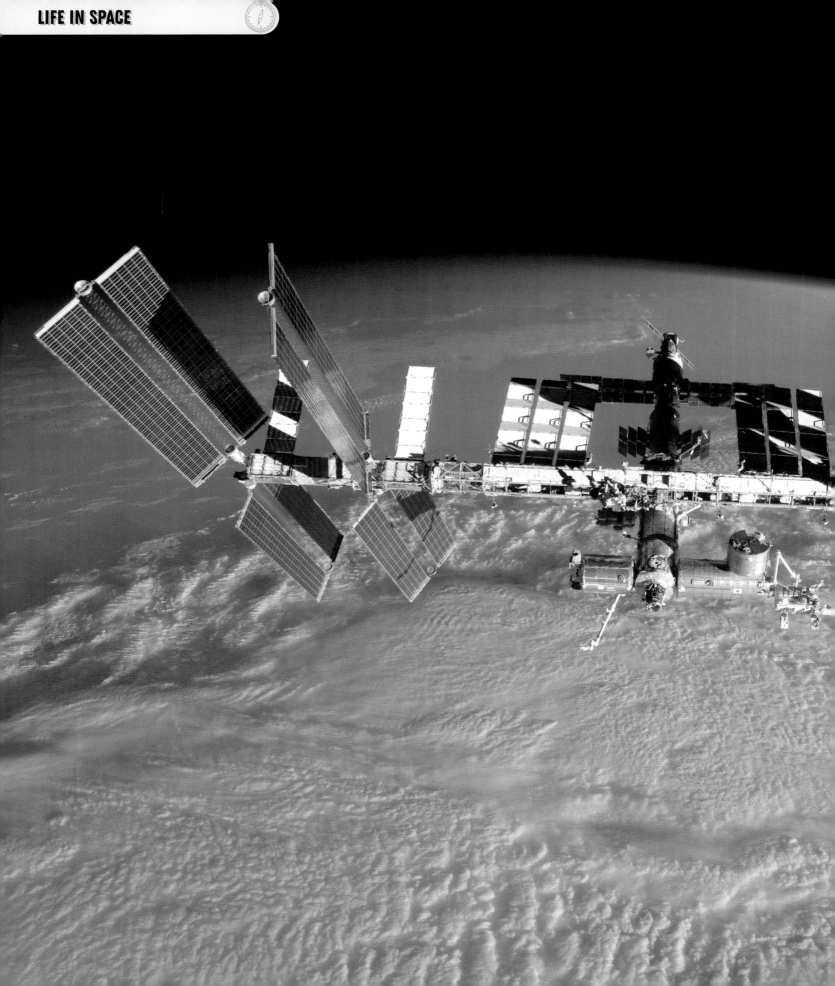

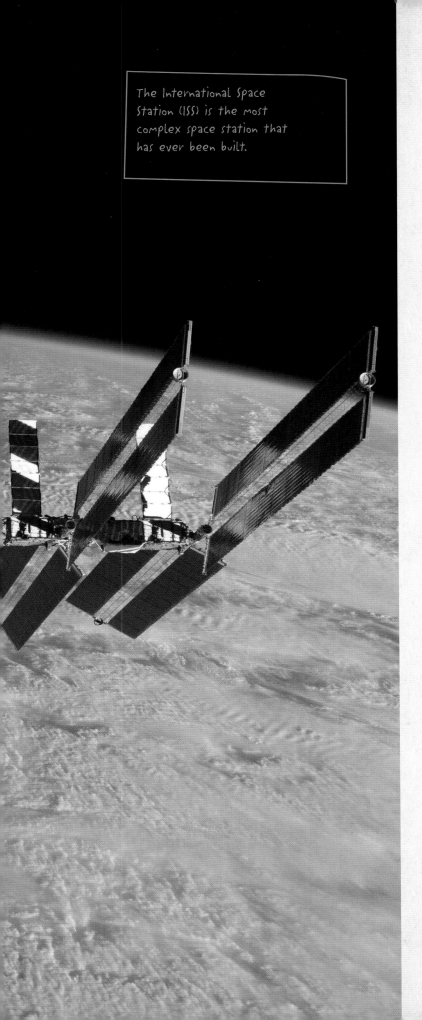

The International Space Station (ISS) is the most complex space station that has ever been built.

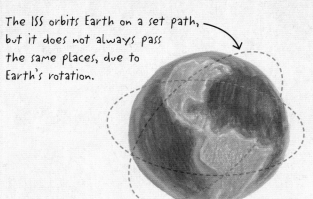

The ISS orbits Earth on a set path, but it does not always pass the same places, due to Earth's rotation.

SPACE STATIONS

Space is a difficult place to get to. Bases called space stations allow astronauts to stay there longer than they could on a spacecraft. Space stations enable astronauts to live above Earth, carrying out detailed experiments. The most famous space station of all is the International Space Station.

The ISS is made up of a number of sections. This picture shows the first two sections being connected in 1998.

41

STAYING IN ORBIT

Only a few space stations have ever been
built. Over time, they have become increasingly
complex, with more room and better facilities.
The result is more astronauts, a greater number
of experiments, and more time spent in space.

Space beds are simply
sleeping bags strapped
to the wall.

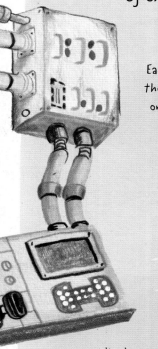

Each astronaut has
their own bedroom
on board, such as
this one.

While in space,
astronauts get
one afternoon off
work each week.

THE INTERNATIONAL
SPACE STATION

A giant laboratory

The ISS was a huge project
that saw 15 countries work
together over 25 years to
build a giant laboratory in
space. The ISS is now the
size of a football field.

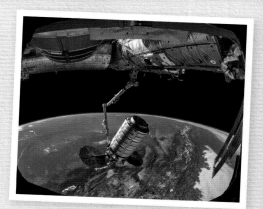

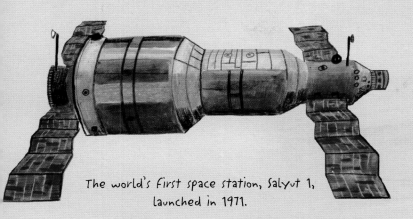

The world's first space station, Salyut 1, launched in 1971.

Salyut

The first ever space station was called Salyut 1. It was very small, with just five small compartments, three of which were for equipment. Although the station was small, astronauts spent 23 days on board, studying the Earth's weather and how their bodies adapted to life in space.

Building space stations

Complex space stations with lots of rooms are created by attaching multiple pieces together. Each room has its own particular purpose. This picture shows the sections of space station Mir.

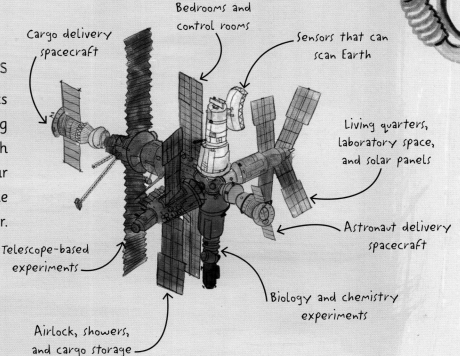

Cargo delivery spacecraft

Bedrooms and control rooms

Sensors that can scan Earth

Living quarters, laboratory space, and solar panels

Astronaut delivery spacecraft

Biology and chemistry experiments

Airlock, showers, and cargo storage

Telescope-based experiments

Frequent flyers

The ISS has a robotic arm to capture spacecraft that want to dock with it. More than 250 people have visited the space station, some of them multiple times.

Keeping busy

Astronauts have carried out more than 3,000 experiments on the ISS! They also do repairs. Here, Scott Parazynski is on a space walk to fix the ISS solar panels.

In preparation to live in space, we have built giant simulated bases on Earth. This base in the Gobi Desert shows what life might be like on Mars.

The Gobi Desert

SPACE BASES

More than 50 years ago, people set foot on the moon. Twelve people spent just a few hours each exploring its surface. We now think we have the technology not just to go back to the moon, but also to spend much longer there and to visit other planets. To do that, we need places to stay.

The Apollo lander was a mini moon base. It could only keep people alive for a couple of days.

HOME FROM HOME

Most places we have discovered in space don't have environments where humans could survive. When we go exploring, we must take vital supplies with us. This can make long stays in these places difficult. A base can provide a safe environment to store materials and keep people healthy.

This image shows what ESA's base could look like under the moon dust.

The base would have rooms to exercise, eat, and sleep.

Moon concrete

The European Space Agency (ESA) plans to "print" a space base, using moon rock to make a special type of concrete. The base will be buried under moon dust, to provide a layer of protection and to trap heat inside.

Recycling

Equipment on a space base is designed to last a long time, and it can often be recycled and reused. The water recycling system on board the ISS recycles 98 percent of the water used, even water from the toilet!

Preparing for the future

Several simulated space bases have been set up to show what it would be like to live off-world. Crews carry out experiments, practice using equipment, and are isolated from everyone except other crewmates.

The Lunares Base in Poland gives astronauts hands-on experience with the difficulties and challenges faced by people trying to live on other worlds.

Some bases have simulated planetary surfaces that are used to test rovers and space suits.

The base would have an airlock, which allows movement between environments.

A space suit would still be required to leave the base.

Some private companies hope to build a settlement on the Red Planet. This is an artist's image of what a base might look like.

Life on Mars

If we can build and operate a base on the moon, Mars may be our next target. We would need lots of resources to be safe on a planet as far away as Mars.

The *Cassini* spacecraft took this image. The pale blue dot below Saturn's rings is Earth.

EARTH

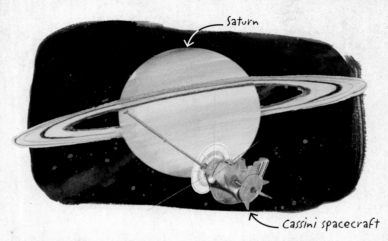

Saturn

← Cassini spacecraft

SOLAR SYSTEM EXPLORATION

An army of spacecraft has explored planets, moons, asteroids, and comets. The many spacecraft send us information, but they also give us perspective, showing how unique, small, precious, and isolated our planet is—Earth is still the only planet that we know of that definitely has life on its surface.

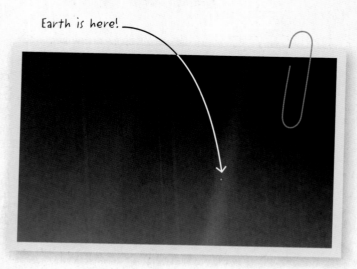

Earth is here!

In 1990, as it sped out of our solar system, NASA's Voyager 1 spacecraft turned its camera back to the Earth and captured our planet as a tiny dot "suspended in a sunbeam."

AMAZING JOURNEYS

Humans have only been exploring space for around 65 years. Since Sputnik 1 became the first satellite to orbit the Earth, we have advanced our engineering skills, solving and uncovering mysteries across the planets.

Four countries have sent missions to the sun.

The moon is the only place other than Earth that humans have set foot.

MOON

Three spacecraft have explored Mercury.

MERCURY

EARTH

SUN

Only half of the over 50 missions to Mars have been successful.

More than 40 missions have visited Venus.

VENUS

MARS

OUTER SPACE EXPLORERS

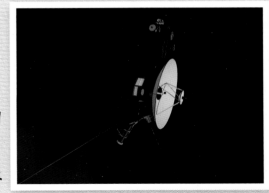

Voyager 1 and 2 are identical spacecraft.

Five human-made spacecraft have been able to leave the solar system, cruising at tens of thousands of miles an hour out into deep space. It will take thousands of years for any of these to reach another star system, but they are humanity's calling card!

JUPITER

There have been 10 missions to Jupiter.

URANUS

Only Voyager 2 has visited Uranus.

PLUTO

New Horizons is the only spacecraft to have visited Pluto.

NEPTUNE

Voyager 2 also did a flyby of Neptune.

ASTEROIDS

Spacecraft have visited nearly 20 asteroids and comets, including Vesta, Eros, Bennu, and Ida.

Five missions have visited Saturn.

SATURN

Pioneer 10 and 11 are also indentical

New Horizons

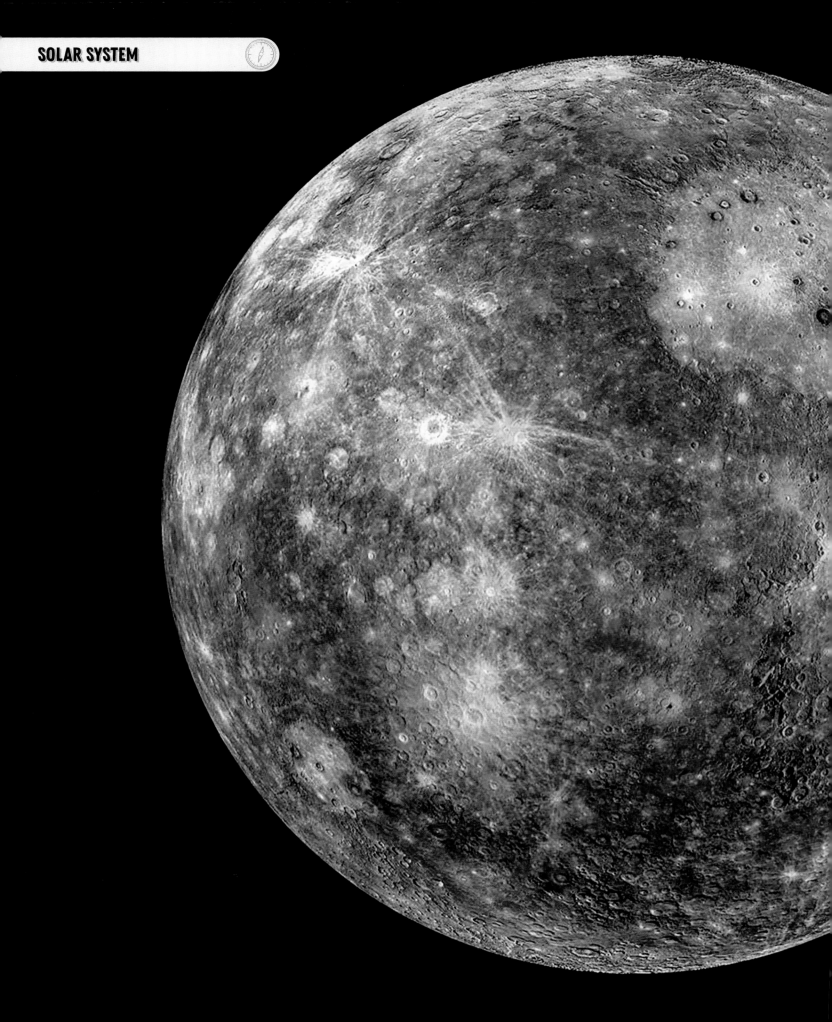

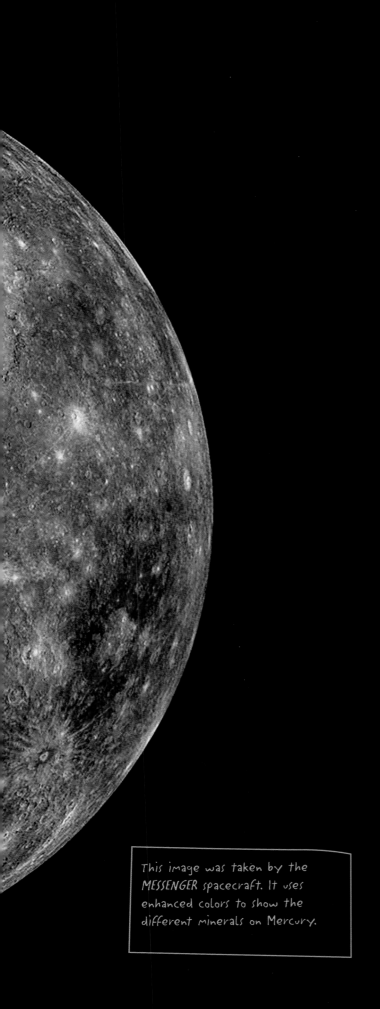

This image was taken by the MESSENGER spacecraft. It uses enhanced colors to show the different minerals on Mercury.

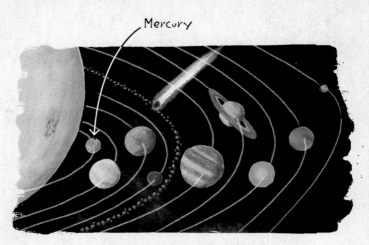

Mercury

MERCURY

Mercury is the closest planet to the sun. It is too hot there for the planet to be able to hold onto gases and have an atmosphere, so it has little protection from meteorites. This means Mercury's surface is littered with impact craters. We still have a lot to learn about this moon-sized planet.

Mercury's Mena crater has "rays" that show where material was blasted out on impact. Over time, the rays will steadily fade away.

SMALL AND MYSTERIOUS

Mercury is still mysterious. Only two spacecraft visited the planet before 2023. A third craft, ESA's *BepiColombo*, aims to unlock more of the planet's secrets.

Freeze or boil

Mercury spins very slowly—one day on Mercury lasts 59 Earth days! It has no atmosphere to trap heat, so the side facing the sun reaches a boiling 806°F (430°C)—more than twice as hot as most ovens! The side facing away from the sun hits a freezing −292°F (−180°C).

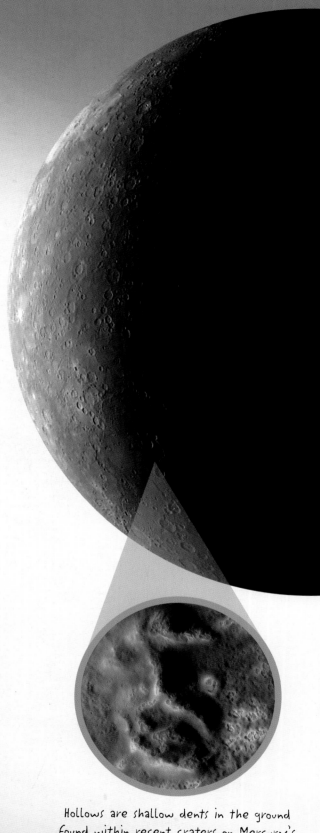

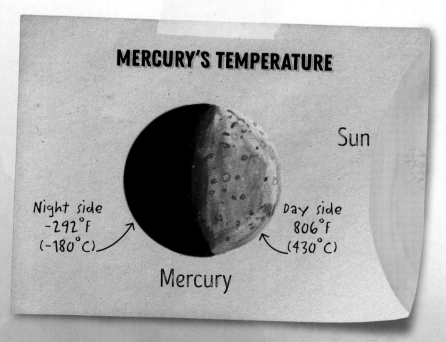

MERCURY'S TEMPERATURE

Sun

Night side
−292°F
(−180°C)

Day side
806°F
(430°C)

Mercury

Hollows are shallow dents in the ground found within recent craters on Mercury's surface. They can be up to a mile wide, and scientists are still trying to figure out exactly what they are!

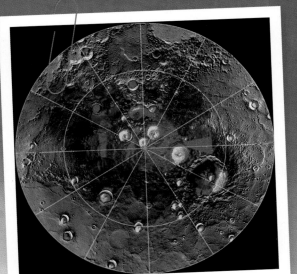

Areas highlighted red here are places where light never reaches and ice could exist.

Ice on Mercury

Liquid water cannot exist on Mercury—it would boil away in the sunlight or freeze instantly in the dark. However, scientists believe that water ice does exist on Mercury, in dark, cold places at the bottom of craters where no light ever reaches.

Difficult to explore

Mercury is difficult to explore because it is so close to the sun. The strong pull of the sun's gravity speeds up spacecraft. When a craft enters orbit around Mercury, it has to use a lot of energy to slow down to keep from being pulled into the sun.

Earth

Venus

Mercury

BepiColombo will use the gravity of Earth, Venus, and Mercury to slow down.

BepiColombo will rely on ion thrusters—electric-powered particle jet packs!

55

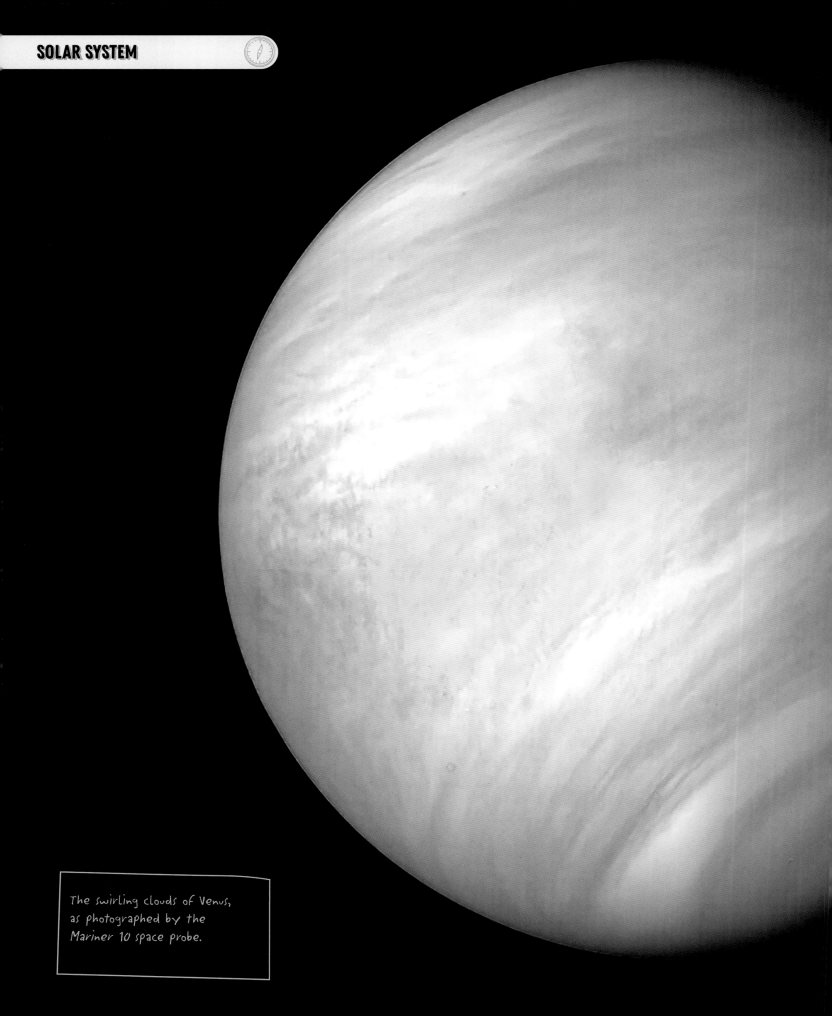

The swirling clouds of Venus,
as photographed by the
Mariner 10 space probe.

Venus

VENUS

The second planet from the sun, Venus is named after the Roman goddess of love. The planet has a beautiful swirling atmosphere, beneath which lies a dangerous land of burning temperatures and acid rain. This makes Venus a very different planet from Earth, despite the two being roughly the same size.

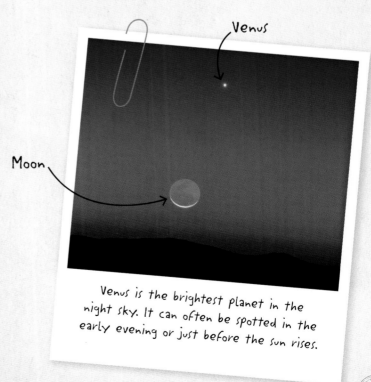

Venus

Moon

Venus is the brightest planet in the night sky. It can often be spotted in the early evening or just before the sun rises.

NEAR NEIGHBOR

Venus passes closer to Earth than any other planet in our solar system. You might think this would make it a good planet to visit and explore. Conditions on the surface of Venus, however, make it difficult for anything to survive there.

The warmest planet

The thick layers of clouds around Venus act as a crushing blanket. They are made of chemicals such as carbon dioxide, the gas we breathe out. Carbon dioxide traps heat, making Venus's surface incredibly hot. Temperatures can reach 860°F (460°C).

This is an artist's impression of the Venera-13 probe, which landed on Venus in 1982. It survived for almost two hours.

Beneath the clouds

The thick clouds of Venus make it tricky for astronomers to see its surface. Early scientists thought that the clouds might come from swamps and that the swamps could have been home to dinosaurs. More recent astronomers have used special radar devices to look through the clouds and have found that the surface is barren and rocky, without a dinosaur in sight.

The Magellan space probe was able to look through the clouds, allowing us to get an idea of what Venus's surface is like.

Life on Venus?

Venus's surface is likely to be too harsh for life to survive there. It's possible, however, that some simple life, such as microbes, might survive in its clouds. NASA is planning to send a new spacecraft named *DAVINCI* to travel through Venus's clouds and learn what chemicals they are made of.

Pancake domes

DAVINCI will travel through Venus's atmosphere, taking pictures and testing the chemicals it finds.

DAVINCI will land, but it is only expected to survive for 18 minutes.

Shield volcanoes

The surface of Venus is covered in volcanoes. Instead of having pointed volcanoes, like some of those on Earth, the volcanoes on Venus are large, round, and flat. They are called shield volcanoes, or pancake domes. Scientists believe the volcanoes are this shape because the lava there is thick and sticky.

VALLES MARINERIS

One of the biggest features on Mars's surface is Valles Marineris, the largest canyon in the solar system.

Mars

MARS

Humans have been obsessed with Mars ever since it was spotted as a red dot in the night sky. Named after the ancient Roman god of war, Mars has been the target of a huge number of robotic missions. As technology improves, scientists hope to one day send humans to visit our neighboring planet.

This photo of the surface of Mars is actually several images pieced together. It shows how the sky color on Mars changes throughout the day. Sunsets are blue due to dust in the sky.

A DESERT PLANET

Like Earth, Mars is a rocky planet with a metal core. However, it is one-and-a-half times farther from the sun than Earth, and about half of Earth's size. Mars has a dry, cold, desertlike surface and no signs of current life.

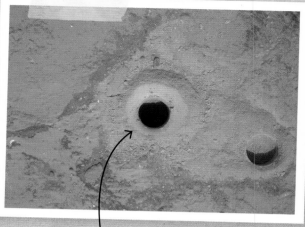

Curiosity drilled into the surface of Mars to reveal Earth-like rock.

Rust surface

The surface of Mars is a distinctive orange—red color. This is due to iron oxide (rust) in the rocks and dust. However, once you go below the surface, the rock looks more like Earth rock, with browns, grays, and blacks.

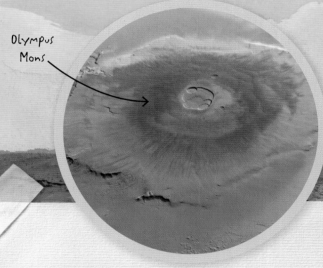

Olympus Mons

Once volcanic

There is lots of evidence to show that Mars was once geologically active, like Earth. Olympus Mons is the biggest volcano in the solar system. It is three times the height of Mount Everest!

Curiosity

NASA's Curiosity rover is the largest rover ever to reach Mars. It was launched in 2011 and landed on Mars in 2012. Curiosity was sent to analyze the climate and geology of Mars. It is still working today, continuing important research, over a decade after it first arrived.

Evidence of water

Today, Mars is dry, but there is plenty of evidence to suggest that it once had liquid water on its surface. Mars has rock types that only form in large bodies of water, and its surface has features similar to Earth's water channels.

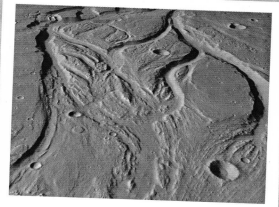

The channels in the image are believed to have been carved by heavy flows of water in Mars's past.

Ingenuity uses solar panels to recharge its batteries.

Ingenuity in flight →

Martian helicopter

Mars's thin atmosphere makes flying on Mars difficult, but not impossible. In 2021, a small helicopter landed on Mars, along with the Perseverance rover. Named Ingenuity, this tiny helicopter became the first human-made object to fly on another planet!

Curiosity rover

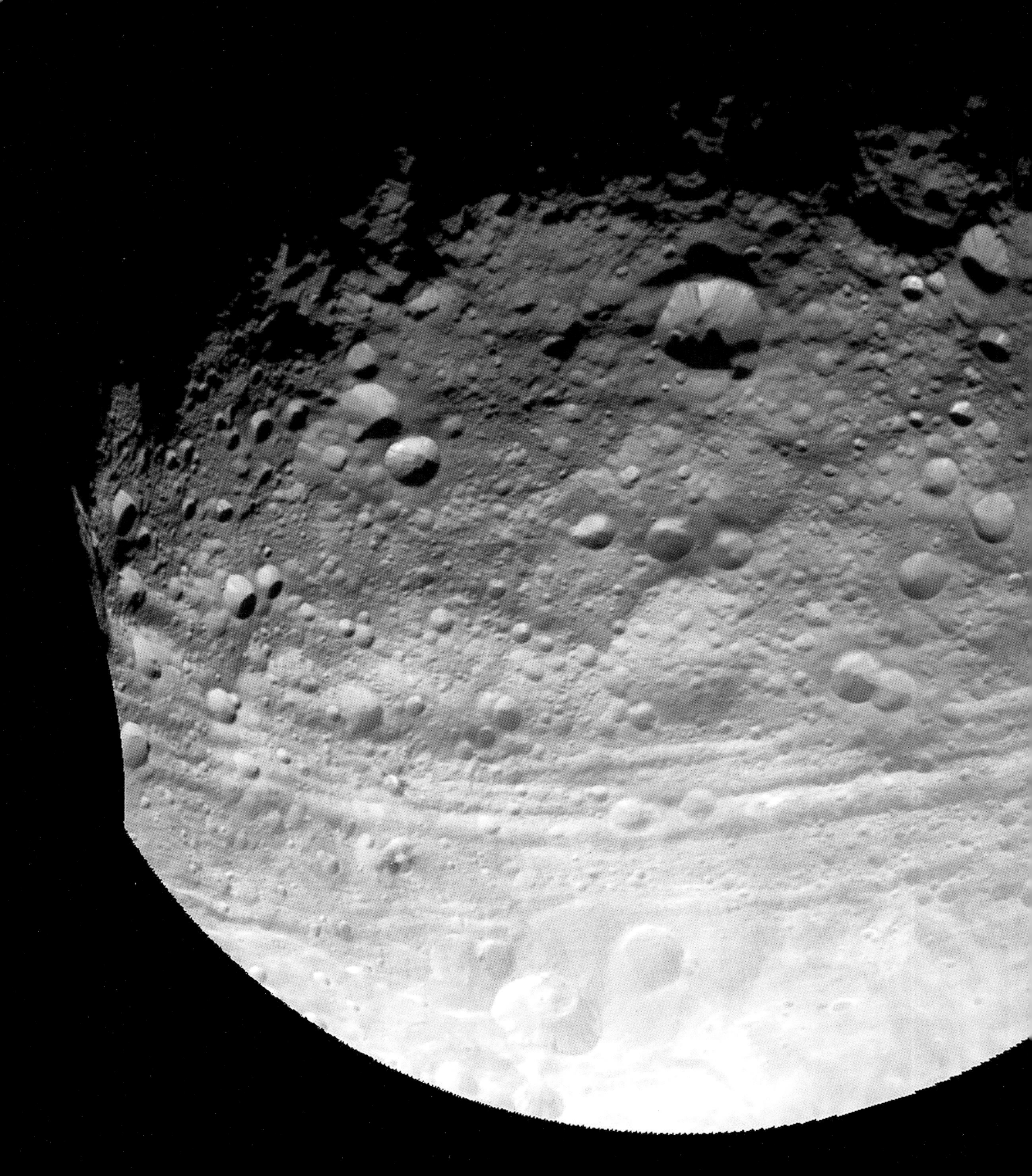

The asteroid belt

ASTEROIDS

These chunks of rock have been drifting through the solar system for millions of years. By number, they are the rulers of the solar system—there are many more asteroids than there are planets. Asteroids come in a range of sizes, from tiny specks of dust to giant hunks of rock that are thousands of miles wide.

Asteroids occasionally bump into planets, leaving pretty big scars! This crater in Arizona was caused by an asteroid colliding with Earth.

This image of the giant asteroid Vesta was taken by the NASA Dawn spacecraft in 2011. Many impact craters can be seen on Vesta's surface.

DRIFTING THROUGH SPACE

Asteroids are material that was left over after the planets formed. There are known to be at least one million asteroids and most are found in the asteroid belt—an area between Mars and Jupiter. However, asteroids are also found throughout the inner solar system.

Finding asteroids

Groups of asteroids are given names based on where they're located. Trojan asteroids "hide" in the orbits of the planets. The bigger the planet, the more Trojan asteroids it tends to have.

The Greek camp, or group, of asteroids orbits in front of Jupiter.

GREEKS

ASTEROID BELT

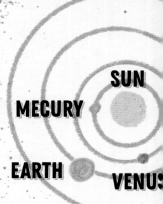

SUN

MECURY

EARTH

VENUS

VESTA

Visiting Vesta

In 2011, NASA's *Dawn* spacecraft visited Vesta, one of the largest-known asteroids. *Dawn* spent just over a year taking detailed pictures and measurements of Vesta. It discovered that Vesta may once have had water on its surface.

HILDAS

As Dawn got closer to Vesta, the pictures it took got better and better.

The Hilda asteroids are a group located beyond the asteroid belt, but inside Jupiter's orbit.

CHARIKLO

JUPITER

Ceres is a dwarf
planet in the
asteroid belt.

The asteroid Chariklo
has rings around it
that are similar
to Saturn's.

CERES

MARS

Kleopatra's moons are called
Alexhelios and Cleoselene.

Special features

Much like planets, some asteroids have
interesting and unusual features. These
include rings and moons. A bone-shaped
asteroid named Kleopatra even has
two moons!

The Trojan camp
of asteroids
follows Jupiter
around the Sun.

TROJANS

Mining in space

Metal is a valuable resource,
and there is likely to be a lot
of metal on some asteroids.
One idea is to mine asteroid
material and bring it back to
Earth, although this would be
extremely difficult to do.

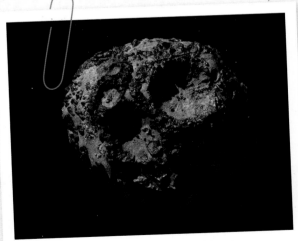

A spacecraft is due to visit the
asteroid Psyche in 2029 to find out
how much metal it contains.

Jupiter

JUPITER

Named after the king of the Roman gods, colossal Jupiter is the largest planet in our solar system. It is also one of the brightest objects in our night sky. Its brightness has led to many years of study, and scientists are still trying to understand this giant planet today.

Jupiter has been studied in detail since the invention of the telescope. This image shows the Great Red Spot, as well as other storms on the surface.

You can often spot Jupiter's largest moons from home using a small telescope or binoculars.

Jupiter

THE BIGGEST OF GIANTS

Unlike Earth, Jupiter is mainly made of swirling gas. This gas was left over after the formation of our sun. Jupiter may have been the first planet to start forming, allowing it to collect large amounts of material as it swept through the early solar system.

Jupiter's outer atmosphere is mainly made up of hydrogen and helium in gas form.

The inner core is likely to contain solid rock, iron, and ice.

The inner atmosphere has even more hydrogen and helium, but in liquid form.

Hydrogen appears in a metallic form in the fluid layer, which allows it to conduct electricity.

Gas giant

Jupiter's gas isn't all wispy and thin. As you get deeper into the gas clouds, gravity squashes the gas more and more. Eventually, the gas gets so thick that it acts more like a thick liquid. Scientists believe that Jupiter even has a small solid core at its center.

Important moons

Jupiter has more than 80 moons. Around 400 years ago, four tiny points of light were spotted close to Jupiter. Astronomers realized that these moons were moving around Jupiter, not Earth. This helped them figure out that the sun was the center of the solar system.

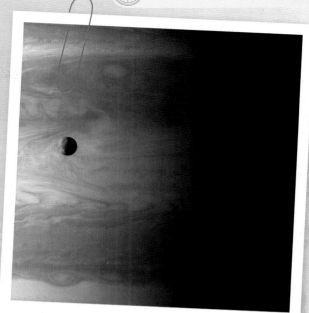

Spacecraft such as Cassini have made it possible for us to see Jupiter's moons in striking detail. This image shows the moon Io passing in front of Jupiter.

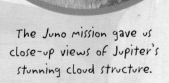

The Juno mission gave us close-up views of Jupiter's stunning cloud structure.

The Juno spacecraft

Endless clouds

Jupiter is a fascinating planet to look at. Its speedy rotation pulls the gas on its surface into a stunning set of swirls and bands. Because Jupiter doesn't have a surface of mountains and valleys, the clouds blow endlessly around the planet.

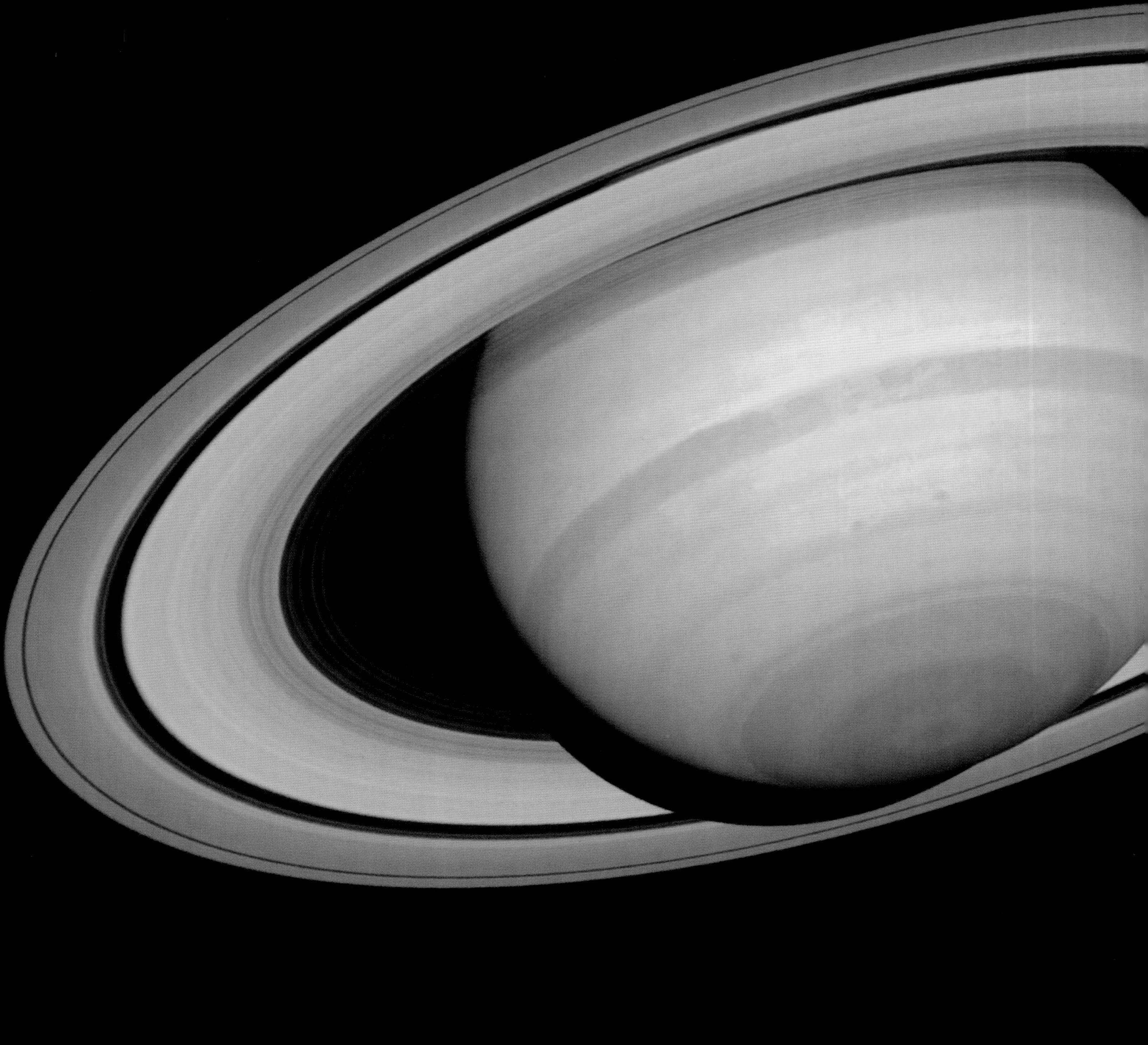

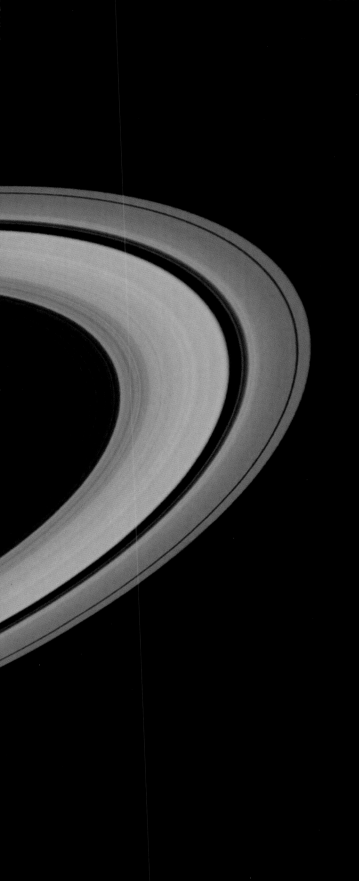

The Hubble Space Telescope took this picture of Saturn in 2004.

Saturn

SATURN

It is only the second-largest planet in the solar system, but Saturn's amazing rings make it remarkable. The planet's mysterious beauty has interested scientists for hundreds of years.

The antenna sends signals back to Earth.

The Cassini space probe spent 13 years orbiting Saturn.

A RINGED GIANT

Saturn is the sixth planet from the sun. It is one of the gas giants, with no solid surface. Galileo Galilei discovered Saturn's rings in 1610, but was unsure exactly what they were. Scientists have only recently been able to answer this question.

Saturn's rings, as captured by the Hubble Space Telescope.

Huge rings

Saturn's amazing rings came as a bit of a surprise to early astronomers. They weren't sure what the rings were, with some even describing them as "ears." Missions to investigate the rings have shown they are actually huge clouds of rock and ice. It is possible the rings were once a giant moon, torn into pieces by Saturn's gravity.

Pan is a moon that orbits inside Saturn's rings. It has collected ring material into a ridge around itself.

Moon helpers

Some of Saturn's 146 moons are found within the planet's rings. Gravity from these moons keeps the rings in shape. Over time, they may grow or be pulled apart and turned into more rings.

Daphnis also orbits inside Saturn's rings. As it moves, it creates waves in the ring material, like the wake of a ship.

Saturn's rings, as seen from Earth. The top picture was taken in December 1994, while the bottom one was photographed in May 1995.

This amazing close-up shows a wisp of rocks and ice being pulled away from the rings.

Wobbly planet

Saturn is a wobbly planet! This affects how much of the rings you can see. At certain points in Saturn's orbit, it wobbles in a way that means we look edge-on at the rings, which makes them almost disappear from sight. At other times, the rings are tilted toward us, and we get an amazing view.

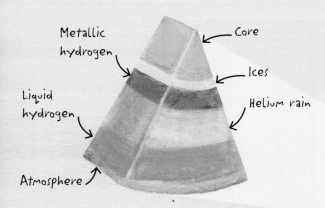

Metallic hydrogen

Core

Ices

Liquid hydrogen

Helium rain

Atmosphere

Measurements show that Saturn would float in water if we could find a bathtub big enough to fit it.

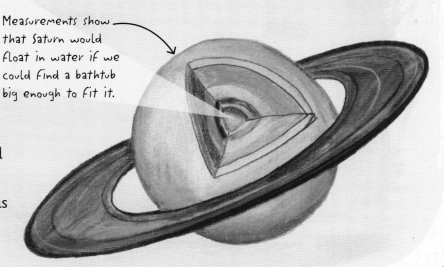

Light, but bulging

Saturn is a peculiar planet. Despite being very large, it is made up of material that is spread out, which makes its density quite low. This light material means that Saturn bulges in the middle as it spins, giving it a slightly squashed-ball shape.

Uranus is so distant that,
so far, only one spacecraft
has been able to reach it.

Uranus

URANUS

This is the seventh planet from the sun, and the farthest planet that can be seen with just the eye. It is so far away that it wasn't recognized as a planet until the 1700s. When William Herschel pointed his telescope at Uranus, scientists were amazed to discover that it was actually a planet and not a star. It became the first planet to be detected using a telescope.

The Voyager 2 probe is the only spacecraft that has visited Uranus. This photo shows engineers preparing it for its epic adventure.

GOD OF THE SKY

Uranus was discovered in the modern era, thousands of years after the other planets. So, it wasn't initially named after a god or goddess. The first name suggested was "King George's Star," after the king of England. However, this name wasn't very popular. It was eventually named "Uranus," after the ancient Greek god of the sky.

Ice giant

Uranus's distance from the sun makes the planet incredibly cold. This has earned it the title of "ice giant." Uranus is likely to be mainly made of water, ammonia, and methane. Recent studies suggest that its makeup may be more liquid or gas than solid.

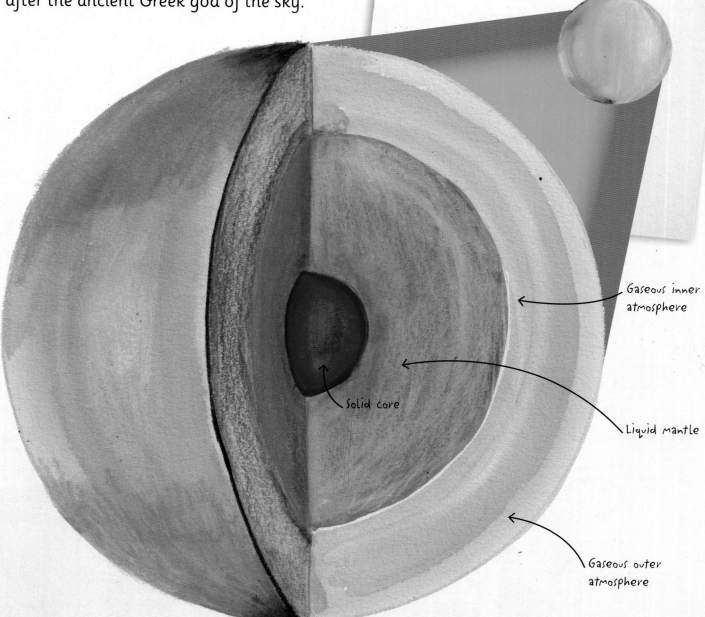

Gaseous inner atmosphere

Solid core

Liquid mantle

Gaseous outer atmosphere

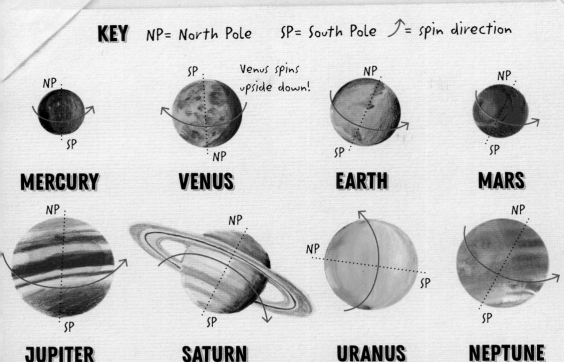

KEY NP= North Pole   SP= South Pole   ↑= spin direction

NP
SP
MERCURY

SP
Venus spins upside down!
NP
VENUS

NP
SP
EARTH

NP
SP
MARS

NP
SP
JUPITER

NP
SP
SATURN

NP
SP
URANUS

NP
SP
NEPTUNE

Sideways planet

One thing scientists quickly noticed about Uranus was that it appears to spin on its side. Most planets spin like spinning tops, with their north poles pointing in roughly the same direction. Uranus is the exception: its north pole points sideways. Because of this, the planet appears to roll around the solar system like a ball.

Extreme seasons

Uranus's toppled-over tilt causes it to experience extreme seasons. The north pole gets constant sunlight for over 40 years, about half of the planet's 84-year orbit. This is likely to power the storms and clouds on Uranus's surface.

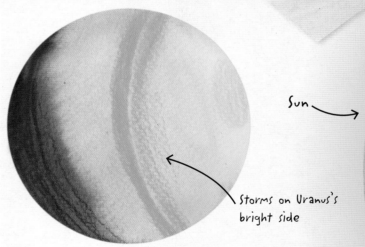

Sun ⟶

Storms on Uranus's bright side

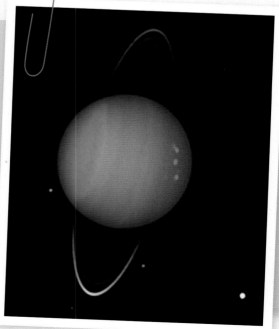

Young rings

When the *Voyager 2* probe flew past Uranus in 1986 it discovered a faint set of rings around the planet. The rings are made of dark material, which makes them difficult to spot. Scientists think the rings are fairly young and may have been created by moons smashing into each other.

This image, taken by the Hubble Space Telescope, shows Uranus's rings. The white dots are some of the planet's moons.

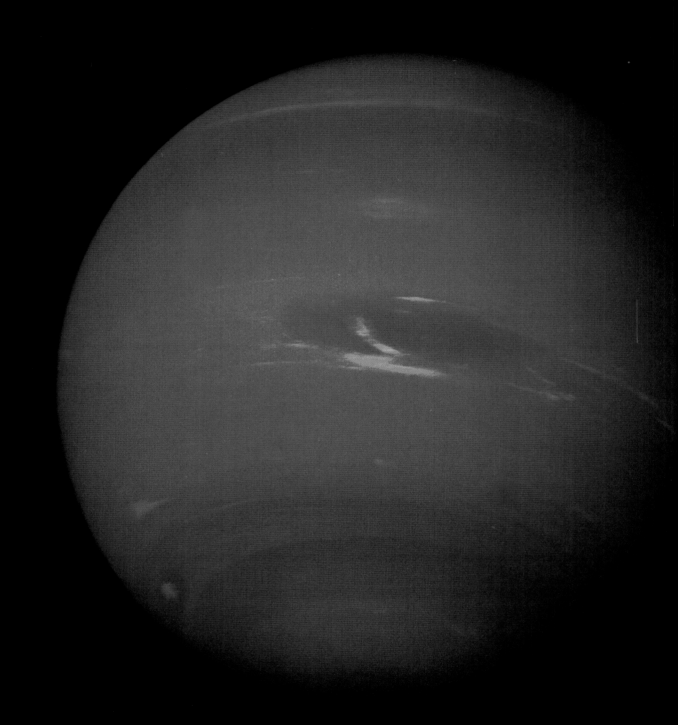

This image of Neptune was captured by the Voyager 2 spacecraft when it flew by the planet in 1989.

Neptune

NEPTUNE

More than 30 times farther from the sun than Earth is, Neptune is the outermost planet in our solar system. Its incredible distance from the sun makes it so dim that it can't be seen from Earth by the human eye—astronomers turned to telescopes to find this mysterious, icy giant.

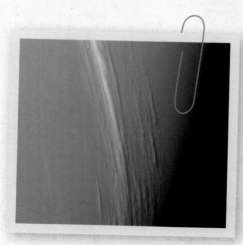

Voyager 2 passed close enough to Neptune to spot bands of clouds at different heights on the planet's surface.

A MYSTERIOUS GIANT

When early astronomers studied the orbits of the
they realized that there should be another large pl
our solar system. In 1846, after predicting where
would be, astronomers peered through their telesc
and found the mysterious eighth planet: Neptune.

Thin rings

A delicate set of rings has been discovered around N
Early calculations suggested that these rings shoul
evened out, but instead formed bands. We now und
it is likely that the gravity from the moon Galatea (i
rings) keeps them pulled into individual bands.

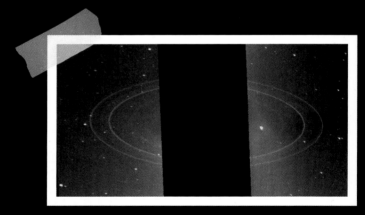

Voya
of Ne
in th
calle
out a
case
see f

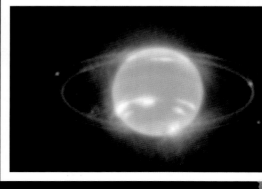

A world of wind

As telescope technology has developed, we have been
able to get startling views of even remote objects, such
as Neptune. We have discovered that Neptune's surface
is covered in weather. It is home to some of the
strongest winds in the solar system,
as well as extensive clouds.

TRITON

At —391°F (—235°C), Triton
has the coldest-known surface
in the solar system.

Neptune has 14 moons that
we know of. The largest, Triton,
orbits Neptune backward when
compared to the other moons.
This makes scientists think that
it may not have formed with the
planet, but was later captured
by Neptune's gravity.

Frozen methane is blown across Neptune's
surface by 1,200-mph (1,900-kph) winds.
These winds often whip the clouds into large,
violent storms. The most famous storm is the Great
Dark Spot. Other storms include a small, speedy bright
storm called Scooter and a dark storm with a light center
called the Wizard's Eye.

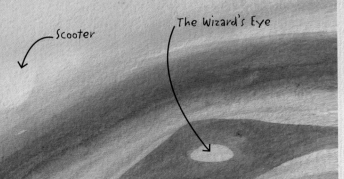

The Great
Dark Spot

Scooter

The Wizard's Eye

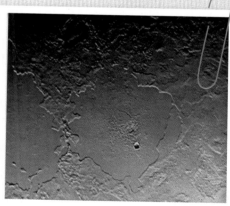

Despite the cold, Triton's surface
shows evidence of flooding,
melting, and eruptions.

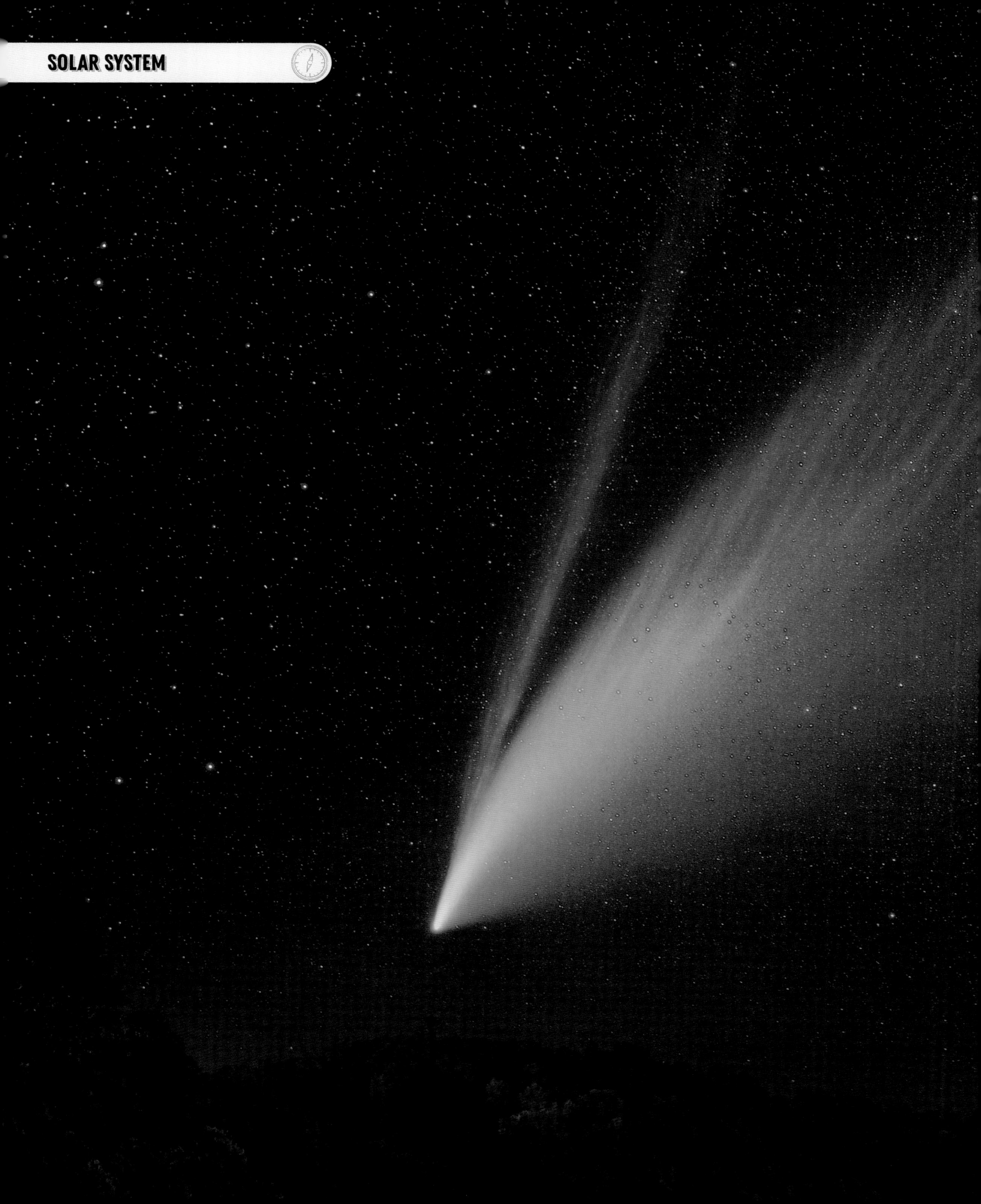

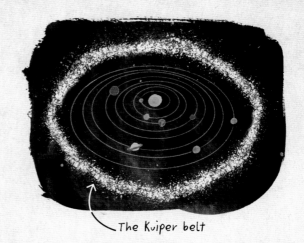

The Kuiper belt

COMETS

Comets are cold balls of dust and ice—
material left over from when our solar
system formed. They spend most of their time
in the Kuiper Belt, far beyond the edge of the
solar system. Others are even further away in
the Oort cloud. Sometimes we see comets in
the night sky, with tails trailing out behind
them as they barrel toward the sun.

Here, comet Neowise flies
across the night sky, its tails
clearly visible.

The Bayeux tapestry includes an image of
Halley's Comet, which was seen the day
before the Battle of Hastings, in 1066.

DISTANT TRAVELERS

Comets have been spotted in our night skies for thousands of years. They were often thought to be signs of bad things to come, or bringers of evil. In recent years, however, we have learned much more about these voyagers of our solar system.

A comet's journey often starts a long way from the sun.

Comet tails

As a comet gets close to the sun it warms up. As it gets hotter, gases inside the comet melt and dust is released from it, giving the comet two tails.

Dust tail
As the comet heats up and starts to thaw, dust that was frozen within it is released.

Ion tail
Some gases get pushed away from the comet by a stream of radiation from the sun called solar wind.

Coma
The layer of gases that form a cloud around the comet.

Nucleus
The solid core of a comet is made of ice, dust, and frozen gases.

The Rosetta Mission

In 2014, the European Space Agency landed a spacecraft on a comet for the first time. It was a bumpy landing, but the Philae lander was able to analyze the comet with a special machine to figure out what it was made of.

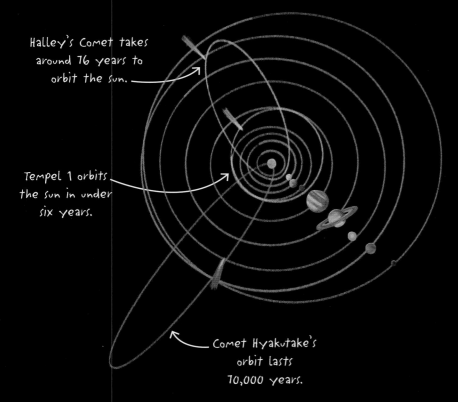

The Philae lander's view of comet 67P's surface.

OTHER COMET FIRSTS

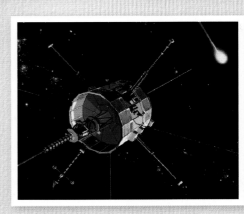

In 1985, the ICE spacecraft flew through the tail of comet P/Giacobini-Zinner.

Halley's Comet takes around 76 years to orbit the sun.

Tempel 1 orbits the sun in under six years.

Comet Hyakutake's orbit lasts 70,000 years.

In 1986, the spacecraft Giotto studied Halley's Comet and made the first close-up observations of a comet nucleus.

Comet journeys

Comets travel in squashed orbits called ellipses. Some, such as the famous Halley's Comet, orbit the sun every hundred years or so. Others take up to tens of thousands of years to make their orbits and travel well beyond the planets.

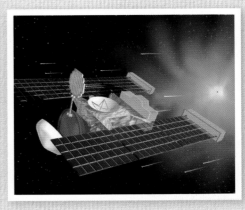

In 2004, NASA's Stardust spacecraft flew behind comet Wild 2, collecting material from the comet.

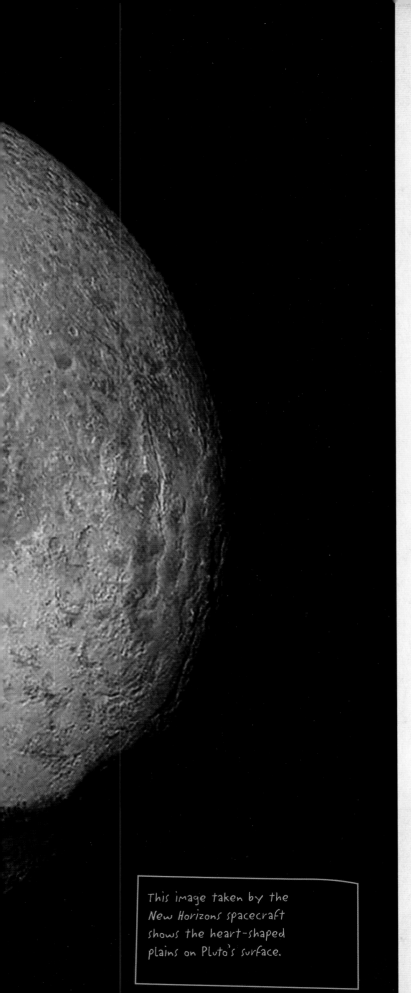

This image taken by the
New Horizons spacecraft
shows the heart-shaped
plains on Pluto's surface.

Asteroid belt

Pluto

DWARF PLANETS

In 2006, it was declared that Pluto was
no longer a planet. Instead, it became known
as a dwarf planet. There are currently five
official dwarf planets. They all orbit the sun,
and some have moons. Dwarf planets are
some of the most interesting objects in
our solar system, despite not being
"real" planets!

The dwarf planets

Eris   Pluto   Haumea   Makemake   Ceres

THE NEARLY PLANETS

Dwarf planets have many of the traits needed to be
a true planet. They are big enough that their gravity has
pulled them into a nearly spherical shape, and they orbit
the sun. However, none of them is big enough that their
gravity has pulled everything in their orbits into them.
This is what stops them from being true planets.

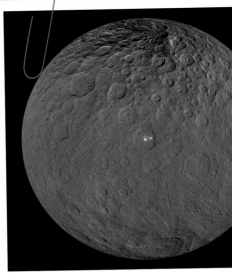

This image of Ceres was taken by
NASA's Dawn spacecraft.

Pluto

Pluto lies at the edge of our solar system
in a region of space called the Kuiper belt.
Pluto is smaller than our own moon and
has its own moons: a large one called
Charon, and four smaller moons that
rotate rapidly. This dwarf planet also has
huge icy mountains, which are probably
floating on a sea of nitrogen ice.

This stunning image of Pluto's
mountains was taken by
NASA's New Horizons
spacecraft.

Under Ceres' surface

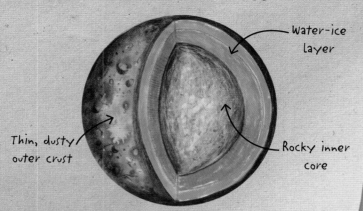

Water-ice layer

Thin, dusty outer crust

Rocky inner core

Ceres

This is the dwarf planet that is closest to us, and the only one found in the asteroid belt. Ceres is much smaller than Pluto and has no moons. There is evidence of liquid water below its surface, which could make it a good candidate for being home to life-forms.

Haumea

Of the five dwarf planets, Haumea is the strangest. Located beyond Pluto in the Kuiper belt, it spins very fast and looks like a giant egg. Haumea has two moons, which were probably formed in a collision with an asteroid many years ago. The same collision likely created Haumea's faint ring.

Comet ISON was discovered in 2012. The details of its orbit suggest it came from the Oort cloud, which is at the very edge of our solar system.

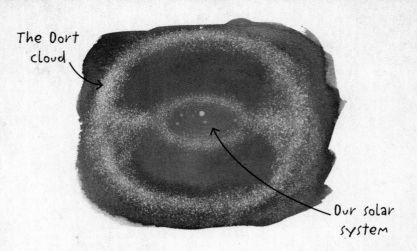

The Oort cloud

Our solar system

THE OORT CLOUD

Lurking out at the very edge of our solar system may be a giant cloud of small icy objects, including comets. This enormous cloud is called the Oort cloud, and it could be the final layer of our solar system. The Oort cloud is very far away from us, but every so often some of its comets come hurtling toward the inner solar system.

Comet McNaught could be seen from Earth in 2007. It seems to have begun its journey beyond the usual starting point of comets in our solar system.

EYOND THE BELT

ny comets start their journeys in the
er belt, just beyond the orbit of Neptune.
ntists noticed, however, that some comets
orbits that suggested they came from much
her away. After studying the data, scientists
d a distant region of space the comets could
e from. It was named the Oort cloud, after the
ch astronomer who did much of the work.

Edge of the solar system

While astronomers haven't yet seen the Oort cloud directly, they are pretty certain that it must exist. Research shows there must be a large cloud containing billions of icy bodies circling around the edge of our solar system. The very edge of this cloud would be the very edge of our solar system.

After 50 years of travel, Voyager 1 has reached the edge of the sun's magnetic field (heliosphere). It will take up to 30,000 more years to clear the Oort cloud and truly leave the solar system.

The planets

Voyager 1

HELIOSPHERE

BUILDING KNOWLEDGE

Armin Leuschner

American astronomer Armin Leuschner started to analyze where distant comets came from. Following this work, Ernst Opik, from Estonia, suggested the idea of the Oort cloud. Jan Oort pulled this work together to show that the Oort cloud probably exists.

Ernst Opik

Causing comets

Most of the time, the icy objects in the Oort cloud are in stable orbits. What knocks them off course and sends them in toward the inner solar system is not fully understood. Scientists think that the passage of nearby stars causes some of the objects to be knocked off course toward the sun.

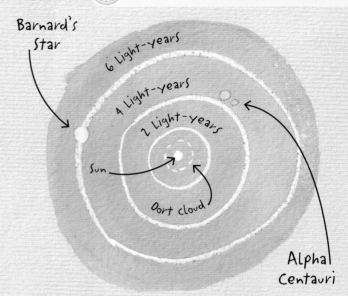

Barnard's Star

6 Light-years

4 Light-years

2 Light-years

Sun

Oort cloud

Alpha Centauri

Other stars in our galaxy, such as Alpha Centauri and Barnard's Star, move around. The gravity of these moving stars could knock Oort cloud objects into new courses, despite being light-years away.

OORT CLOUD

Interstellar object

In 2017, astronomers detected an object that may have come from even farther than the Oort cloud. 'Oumuamua was a long, rocky object spotted flying through our solar system. It is now thought that this may be the first confirmed object that has come from another solar system.

An artist's impression of what we think 'Oumuamua looks like.

Jan Oort

The sun is made of superhot gases known as plasma. As the plasma heats up and cools, it rises and falls, creating pockets on the surface called granules (pictured).

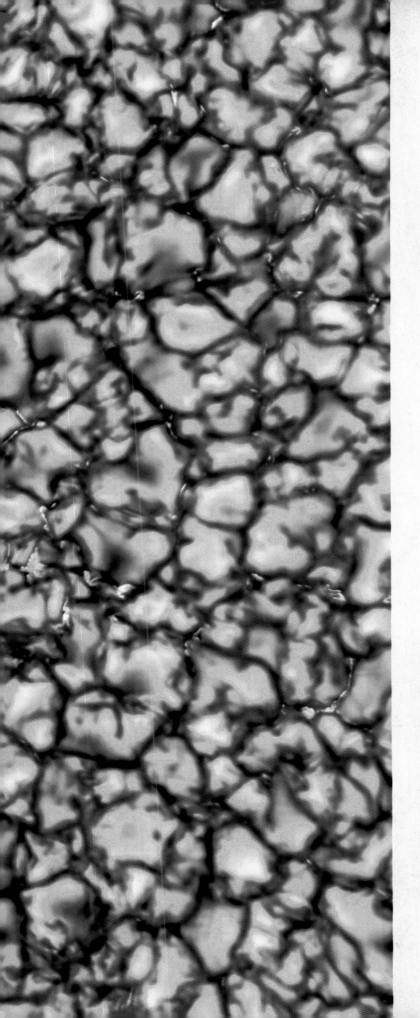

The sun

THE SUN

The sun is a star—a giant, superhot ball of gas. It produces all of the light and heat that is needed for life to survive on our planet. The sun contains most of the mass of the solar system and sits in its center—the sun's gravity keeps everything else in the solar system locked in orbit around it.

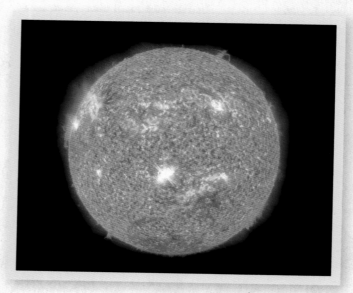

The sun is almost 800,000 miles (1.4 million km) wide and could fit 1.3 million Earths inside it.

HUGE ENERGY

The sun produces energy through a process called fusion. Hydrogen gas is smashed together, making helium gas. This releases heat energy. The surface of the sun is 10,472°F (5,800°C)—about 300 times hotter than a kitchen oven. Its core is about 59 million °F (15 million °C)!

Like the planets, the sun is made up of many layers.

Solar flare

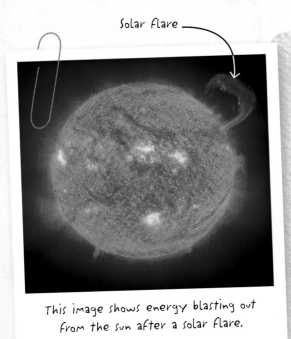

This image shows energy blasting out from the sun after a solar flare.

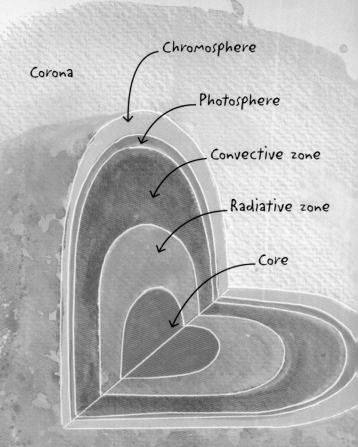

Corona

Chromosphere

Photosphere

Convective zone

Radiative zone

Core

Energetic ejections

The sun has strong magnetic fields that cause darker areas, called sunspots, to form on its surface. Sometimes, these areas will suddenly get brighter, releasing a large amount of energy in an event called a solar flare. The energy released can be greater than that of a million nuclear bombs going off and can throw material from the sun into space.

Only the hazy ring of the sun's corona can be seen during a total solar eclipse.

Eclipses

The moon is just the right size that if it passes between Earth and the sun at the right angle, it can block the sun. This is called a solar eclipse. If the sun is completely covered, we call it a total eclipse. When this happens, the birds stop singing and everything gets cooler and quieter.

Sun

Earth

Moon

A solar eclipse occurs when the moon passes between Earth and the sun.

Never look directly at the sun!

Our sun is fascinating, and it can be tempting to look up at it, but it is so bright that if you do, you can permanently damage your eyes. You can look at the sun safely using special filters or a pinhole camera.

A view of a partial eclipse using a simple pinhole camera.

Light passes through the small "pinhole" and is projected onto paper.

We can see Earth's moon
every night. It is an
incredible sight!

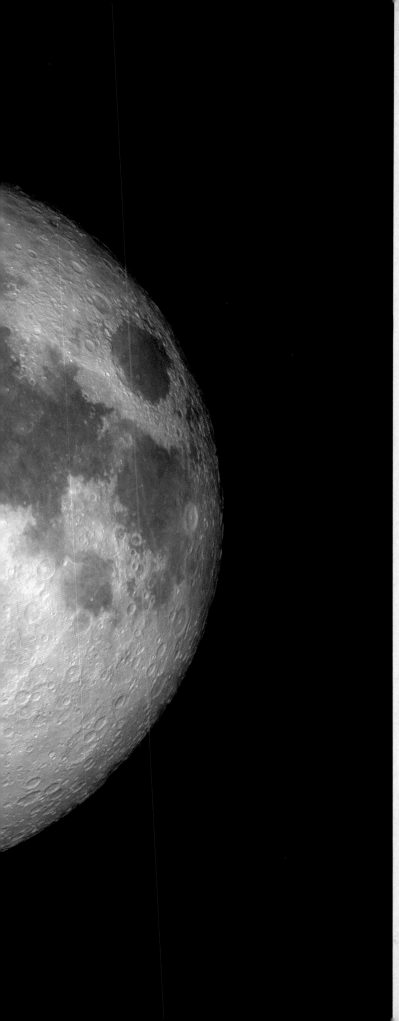

Our moon orbits Earth

MANY MOONS

When we think about our solar system, we tend to focus on the planets. However, there are more than 200 moons orbiting around the planets, and some of them are pretty amazing.

Because of the way the moon orbits, we only ever see one side of it. This picture shows the far side of the moon, which we can't see from Earth.

PLANETS' COMPANIONS

There are some weird and wonderful moons in our solar system. Let's leave the planets behind and see what we can learn about the solar system from their companions.

The mighty Ganymede is so big that if it orbited the sun instead of Jupiter it would be called a planet.

The biggest moon

Ganymede is the largest moon in the solar system. It is bigger than Mercury, and almost as big as Mars. It is so big that it has a magnetic field that creates auroras similar to those seen on Earth.

The Hubble Space Telescope detected glowing auroras in Ganymede's atmosphere.

Moonshine

Saturn's moon Enceladus is the most reflective object in the solar system, because it is covered in a thick layer of ice. This ice is churned up from a huge underground ocean. Water sprays up from geysers and then freezes on its surface, making it super shiny!

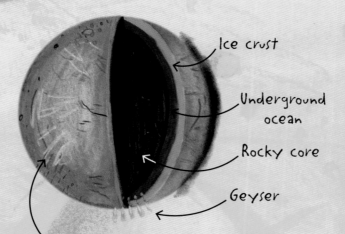

Ice crust

Underground ocean

Rocky core

Geyser

The thick ice crust has cracks and valleys, suggesting that its surface is constantly changing. There may even be life swimming in these oceans.

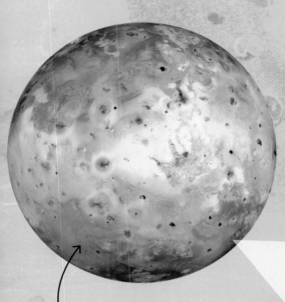

Volcanic Io

Io is the moon closest to Jupiter. It's constantly squashed and squeezed by Jupiter's gravity, making it the most volcanic object in the solar system—there are more than 400 volcanoes on its surface! Some of Io's volcanoes are taller than Mount Everest, on Earth. Io is covered in a chemical called sulfur, giving it a yellow color.

Io's volcanoes constantly churn new material onto its surface, giving it a strangely smooth look.

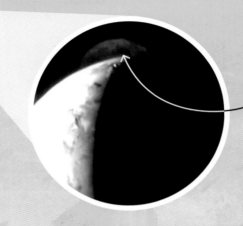

The *New Horizons* spacecraft captured this huge volcanic eruption on the surface of Io. Material was thrown 200 miles (330 km) into the air!

Making a moon

Studies of our own moon have shown that it contains rocks very similar to those found on Earth. This suggests that while Earth was fairly new, a large object collided with it, knocking debris into space. This debris was captured in Earth's gravity and became the moon.

Moon

Theia

Earth

Debris comes together

Impact

Disk of debris

This Great White Spot was more than 6,000 miles (9,500 km) wide. That's bigger than the distance between London, UK, and Perth, Australia.

Great White Spot

SPACE WEATHER

When we check a weather report,
we learn about weather on Earth.
However, weather is found in lots of places
throughout the solar system. Some of the
wildest weather comes in the form of storms,
such as Saturn's Great White Spot.

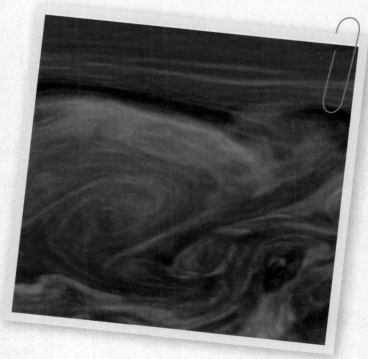

This image uses different colors
to show cloud patterns during
a Great White Spot.

WILD WIND AND RAIN

Extreme types of weather have been found on planets and moons throughout the solar system. From planet-sized winds to diamond rain, space weather can be truly wild. Space weather probably doesn't end with our nearest neighbors—scientists think weather is likely to exist throughout the universe.

Giant storms

Saturn and Jupiter are known as gas giant planets. As they rotate, their gassy surfaces swirl, creating giant storms. One of the most famous storms is Jupiter's Great Red Spot, an enormous hurricane that has been raging for more than 350 years.

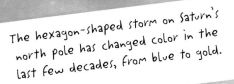

The hexagon-shaped storm on Saturn's north pole has changed color in the last few decades, from blue to gold.

Earth

Jupiter

Jupiter's Great Red Spot is 1.3 times the width of Earth.

Diamond rain

Scientists think that the clouds above Uranus probably contain diamonds instead of water. They are likely to be pretty big diamonds, too—each one would be the size of a blue whale!

It is difficult to know what happens below Uranus's atmosphere, but laboratory experiments suggest diamond rain does exist.

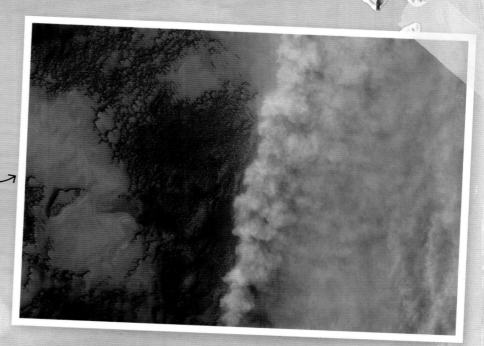

A dust storm sweeping across the surface of Mars.

A dust devil, caused by warm air rising and collecting sand.

Dangerous dust

On the rocky planets, such as Mars, weather takes a different form. Mars has little gravity, which means wind can blow up even more dust than on Earth. Scientists have found huge dust storms, which sometimes cover the whole planet! Tracking these storms is important, since they can damage visiting missions.

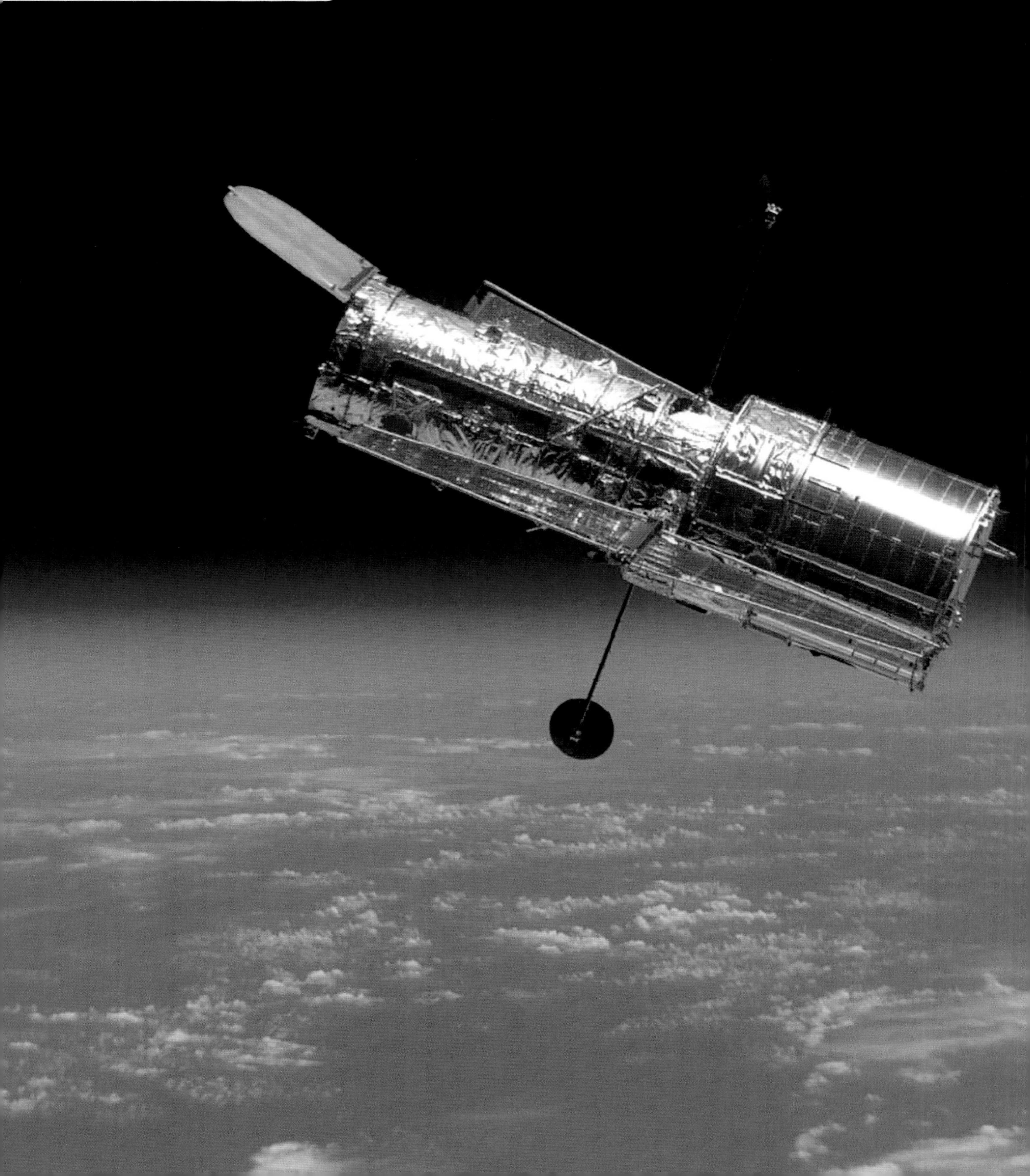

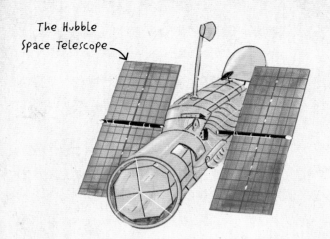

The Hubble
Space Telescope

The Hubble Space Telescope
was launched into space in
1990. It gives us incredibly
clear views of deep space.

LOOKING INTO SPACE

Humans have been looking into space for
thousands of years. Ancient cave paintings
show that our ancestors were amazed by the
stars and attempted to understand what they
meant. As time has passed, we have continued
this interest and have become better at looking
into the universe and understanding it.

In 1668, Sir Isaac Newton used a telescope much
like this one. Telescope technology has come
a long way in the last 400 years!

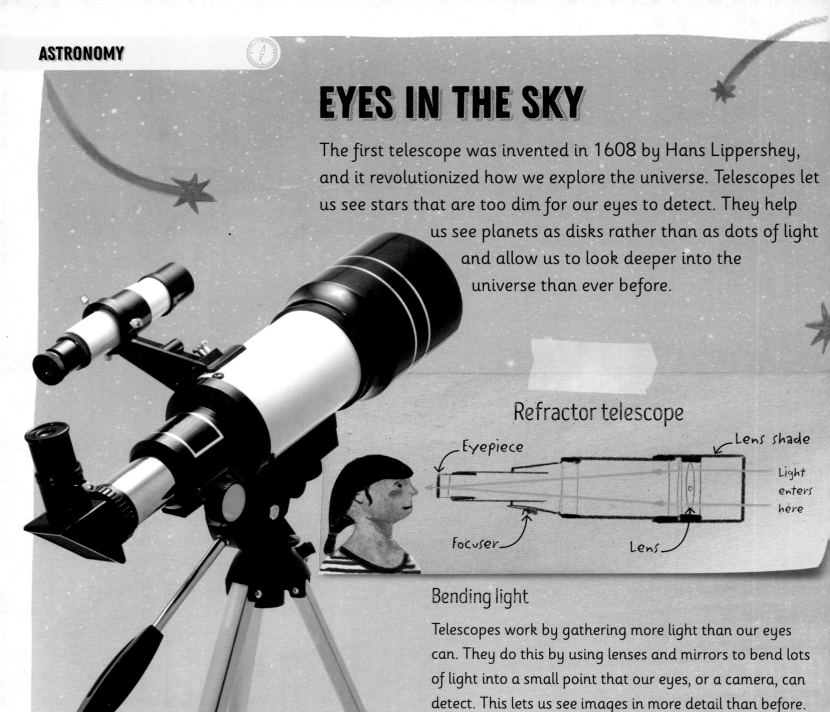

EYES IN THE SKY

The first telescope was invented in 1608 by Hans Lippershey, and it revolutionized how we explore the universe. Telescopes let us see stars that are too dim for our eyes to detect. They help us see planets as disks rather than as dots of light and allow us to look deeper into the universe than ever before.

Refractor telescope

Eyepiece

Lens shade

Light enters here

focuser

Lens

Bending light

Telescopes work by gathering more light than our eyes can. They do this by using lenses and mirrors to bend lots of light into a small point that our eyes, or a camera, can detect. This lets us see images in more detail than before.

SPECIALIZED TELESCOPES

Astronomers use lots of different telescopes in their exploration of space. They often have unique jobs and use different tools.

TESS

TESS looks for planets orbiting around other stars. These planets are called exoplanets. TESS will monitor more than 200,000 stars for signs of exoplanets.

Seeing stars

Bigger and better telescopes help us to see clear pictures of deep space. But down here on Earth, the atmosphere makes things tricky. If you've ever looked at the stars on a clear night, you will notice that they twinkle. However, the stars themselves aren't shimmering and changing brightness. This effect is caused by the air in our atmosphere wobbling the light on its way to our eyes. Astronomers call this "seeing."

↖ Star

Shorter path, less twinkling

Longer path, more twinkling

Atmosphere

The stars appear to twinkle due to the same effect that makes things look bent when put in water.

Space telescopes

To stop Earth's atmosphere from making our images look blurry, we started launching telescopes into space. Space telescopes can be used all the time, without having to wait for the sun to go down. The Hubble Space Telescope has taken more than 1.5 million pictures.

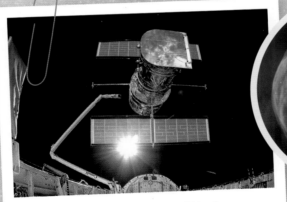

This image shows the Hubble Space Telescope being launched by the Space Shuttle Discovery, in 1990.

Hubble captured this amazing image of the Bubble Nebula on its 26th birthday.

Euclid

Euclid is looking for a mysterious material called dark matter. It will observe billions of galaxies, some of which are 10 billion light-years away.

Planck

The Planck Telescope studied a type of light called microwaves. It was launched in 2009 and studied the skies for four years.

This is how the constellation Orion looks in real life, viewed from Earth.

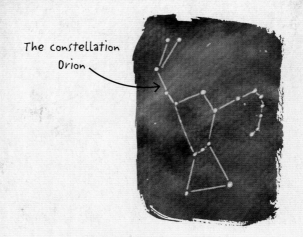

The constellation Orion

CONSTELLATIONS

Constellations are groups of stars in the night sky. For thousands of years, humans have seen images in these groups and given them names associated with myths and legends. People also used constellations to help them find their way when sailing across open seas.

The ancient Greeks named the constellation Orion after a famous hunter whose image they saw outlined in the stars.

FAMOUS TALES

There are 88 officially recognized constellations. Most of them are named after characters from ancient Greek and Roman stories, although other cultures also have stories about them. Astronomers use constellations as signposts, to help them find objects in the night sky.

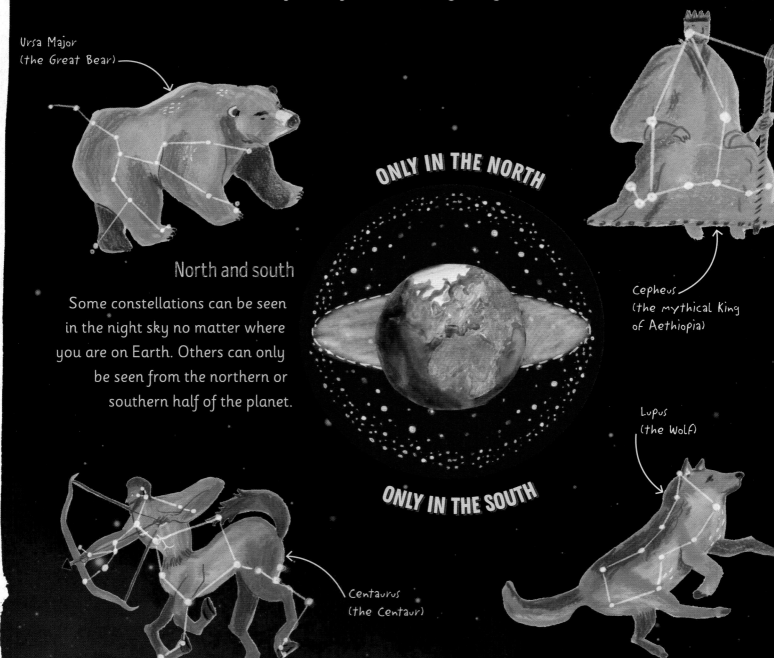

Ursa Major
(the Great Bear)

ONLY IN THE NORTH

Cepheus
(the mythical King
of Aethiopia)

North and south

Some constellations can be seen in the night sky no matter where you are on Earth. Others can only be seen from the northern or southern half of the planet.

ONLY IN THE SOUTH

Lupus
(the Wolf)

Centaurus
(the Centaur)

This image was taken over many hours. The circular tracks show the stars moving as Earth spins. The star in the center that doesn't move is the North Star.

MAPPING SPACE

The constellations are used to map space. Astronomers imagine a "celestial sphere"—a bubble around Earth that is divided into the 88 constellations. The constellations can then be used to position other objects in space.

Orion is a huge constellation containing many objects.

The North Star

Because Earth is spinning, the stars seem to move across our night sky. That is except for one, the North Star. This star sits directly above the North Pole, so the spinning of Earth doesn't affect where we see it. Because it doesn't move, ancient explorers used the North Star to find the direction of north.

The Flame Nebula is in the "hip" of Orion's belt.

A meteor creates a glowing streak as it enters Earth's atmosphere during the Perseid meteor shower.

Meteor falling to Earth

METEORS

Every year, an estimated 25 million pieces of space rock and debris fall toward Earth. Most of them don't make it all the way down to Earth's surface—they burn up in a spectacular light show as they enter our atmosphere. These streaks of burning rock are called meteors.

This combined image shows the Geminid meteor shower, which occurs every year in December.

CRASH COURSE

We often think of space as being empty, but it still contains plenty of matter, such as dust and rocks. As our planet orbits around the sun, it occasionally ends up on a collision course with some of this material. When this dust and rock collides with our atmosphere it heats up and glows, creating meteors.

Naming rocks

Rocks from space are named according to where they are. While they are in space, before they reach our atmosphere, we call them meteoroids. Meteors are rocks in the Earth's atmosphere. If meteors make it to the ground, we call them meteorites.

Showers

Meteors can come from any rock or debris in space. However, many of them come from the trails of comets. As comets travel through the solar system, they leave clouds of rock behind them. If these clouds cross Earth's orbit, they create a meteor shower every time Earth passes through their trail. This is why we have regular meteor showers every year, as well as random meteors appearing at other times.

Comet 73P/Schwassmann—Wachmann broke up, leaving a large trail of rocky fragments. Events like this leave clouds of material, which can then cause meteor showers.

SPACE

Meteoroid

ATMOSPHERE

Meteor

EARTH

Meteorite

Meteorites can be split into three main types,
depending on how much iron and nickel they contain.

Stony meteorite

Stony meteorites
are called
chondrites. They
are the most
common meteorite and
are made of tiny fragments
squashed together.

Iron meteorite

Iron meteorites
contain nickel and
iron. They make up
around 5 percent of
all meteorites and have a
metallic look. Iron meteorites
are made mostly of metal.

Pallasite meteorite

The rarest type of
meteorites are called
pallasite meteorites. In
these, rocky crystals
are mixed in with
the metal, creating
stunning patterns.

The smoothed fusion
crust is slightly chipped,
revealing the rougher
surface beaneath.

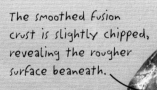

Identifying meteorites

Figuring out if a rock could be from
space is a tricky task, and often needs
to be confirmed in a laboratory.
One good clue can be if the rock has
a smoothed surface, called a fusion
crust. This forms when the rocks are
heated by Earth's atmosphere.
Many meteorites are also magnetic.

This stunning image from the
Webb Telescope shows us some
galaxies that existed around
13 billion years ago.

11.3 billion years ago

12.6 billion years ago

13.0 billion years ago

13.1 billion years ago

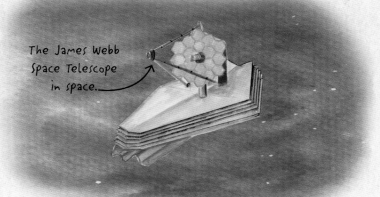

The James Webb Space Telescope in space.

LOOKING INTO THE PAST

Looking into space helps us see and understand the universe around us. Space is so big that studying the light of our universe allows us to peer deep into its history. This is because the light takes time to travel to us. Many of the things we can see now appear as they were a long time in the past, when the light left them.

When we see the moon, we actually see how it looked approximately one second ago.

TRAVELING FAR

Space is enormous. The distances between objects can be millions of miles. Traveling these huge distances can take years, even if you travel incredibly quickly. The fastest moving thing in our universe is light, which travels at 186,000 miles per second (300,000 km per second). But even light from our own solar system doesn't reach us right away.

Delayed image

Because of the incredible size of our universe, whenever we look at something in space, our eyes are seeing the light that left that object a long time ago. For example, the sunlight that is shining on you now left the sun eight minutes ago.

Sun

8 mins

35 mins

Mercury

Venus

Earth

Mars

If the sun stopped shining, we wouldn't know about it for eight minutes!

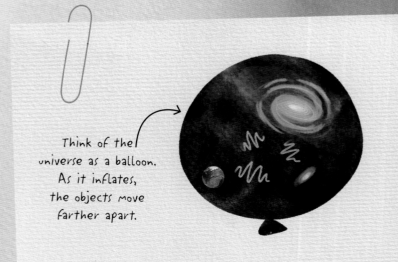

Think of the universe as a balloon. As it inflates, the objects move farther apart.

Light-years

Once we start looking at objects outside of the solar system, the time delay rapidly increases. The second-closest star to Earth, Proxima Centauri, is 4.2 light-years away. This means that it takes the light from Proxima Centauri just over four Earth years to reach us. A light-year is 5.9 trillion miles (9.5 trillion kilometers).

Betelgeuse is a star that is probably going to explode soon. However, since it's 642 light-years away, this may have already happened and we're just waiting for the light to reach us.

4 hours

Jupiter

Saturn

Uranus

Neptune

Red shift

Light takes a long time to travel across space, and it also gets changed during this epic journey. The universe is expanding. Because of this expansion, as light travels through space, the waves that it is made of get stretched. The waves become longer, making much of the light appear redder than usual. This is called red shift.

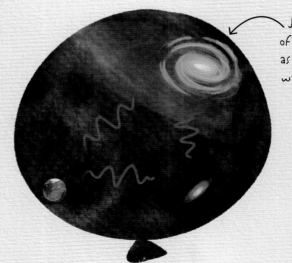

Just as the surface of a balloon stretches as it inflates, so light waves stretch as the universe expands.

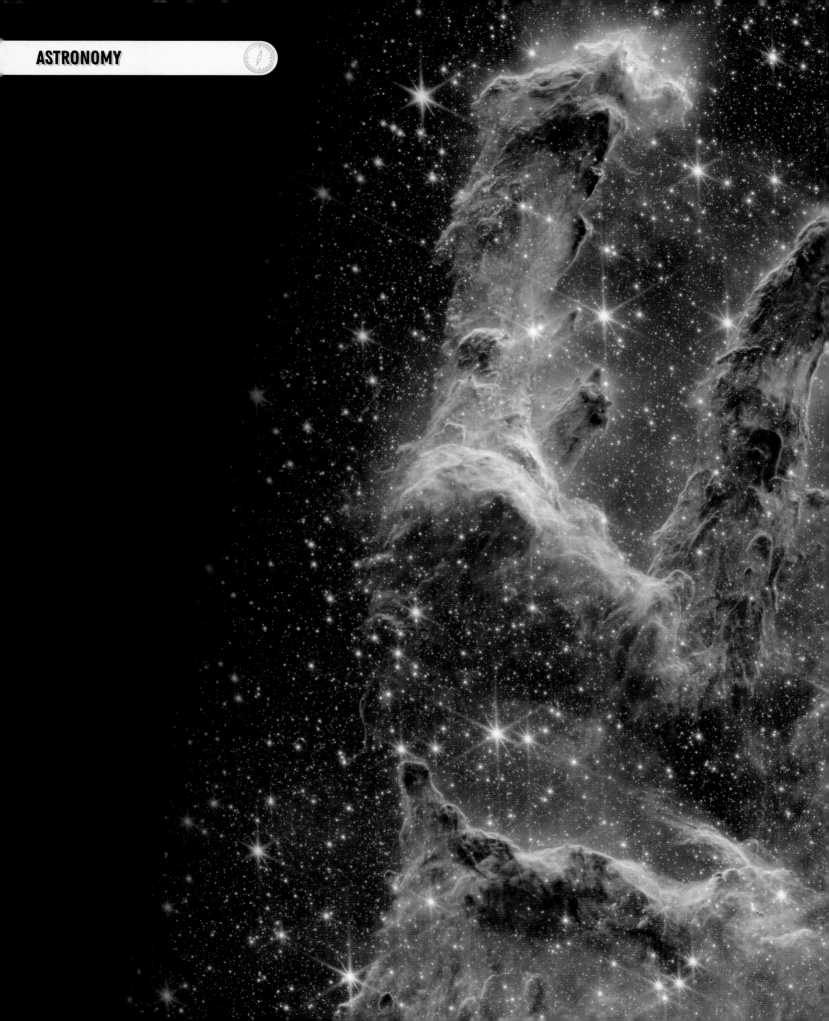

This is an infrared image of part of the Eagle Nebula known as the "Pillars of Creation." It was taken by the James Webb Space Telescope.

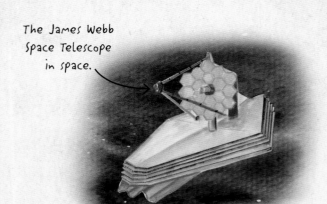

The James Webb Space Telescope in space.

DIFFERENT LIGHT

When we see a rainbow in the sky, we are seeing white light split into all the different colors that make it up. Just as there are different colors of light that we can see, there are different types of light that we can't see. These different types of light can show us a lot about space.

This image also shows the Pillars of Creation, but taken by the Hubble Space Telescope using visible light.

"SEEING" THE LIGHT

We can't see different types of light, but we can sense them. We feel infrared as heat and can get a sunburn from high-energy ultraviolet light. Building telescopes that can detect other types of light allows us to create new images of objects, which tell us more about them.

The spectrum

The range of lights is called the electromagnetic spectrum. Just like a rainbow is a spectrum of visible light, the electromagnetic spectrum is split into different types of light. The shorter the wavelength, the higher the energy.

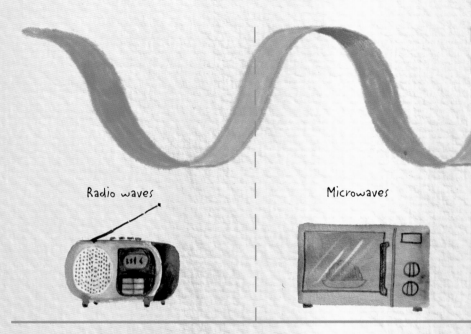

Radio waves

Microwaves

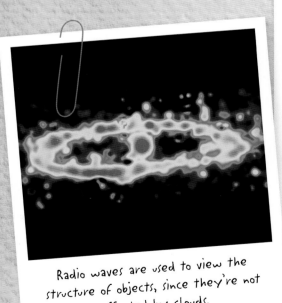

Radio waves are used to view the structure of objects, since they're not affected by clouds.

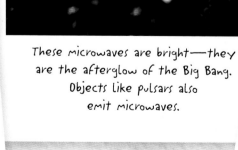

These microwaves are bright—they are the afterglow of the Big Bang. Objects like pulsars also emit microwaves.

Infrared waves can cut through all but the most dense regions of dust in space.

This is what we can see with the naked eye.

X-rays are high in energy and are used to photograph bones.

Gamma rays have the most energy of all the waves. They're made by the hottest objects in the universe.

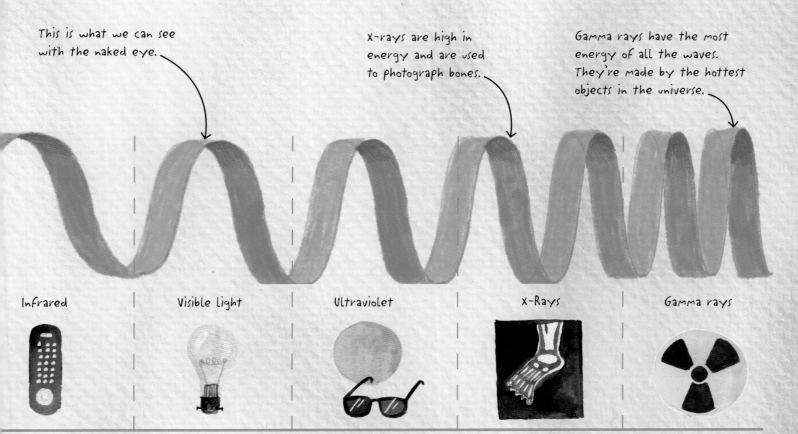

Infrared

Visible Light

Ultraviolet

X-Rays

Gamma rays

Andromeda Galaxy in different lights

The Andromeda Galaxy is our nearest neighboring galaxy. Being so close makes it a perfect target to study. These images show Andromeda in the full range of different lights.

X-rays (pictured) and gamma rays come from the hottest objects and are used to capture images of exploding stars.

This is what we'd see with the naked eye, but these images miss some key details.

Ultraviolet can show some amazing events in space.

Ultraviolet means "beyond violet," as it's beyond visible purple in the electromagnetic spectrum.

Here, the James Webb Space Telescope is being loaded into a test chamber. There were many tests to make sure it could survive in space.

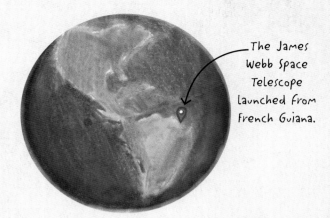

The James Webb Space Telescope launched from French Guiana.

THE JAMES WEBB SPACE TELESCOPE

The James Webb Space Telescope is the biggest, most complicated space telescope ever launched. To design, build, and launch it took more than 30 years of planning and involved thousands of people from all over the world. The Webb Telescope is now out in space, sending back amazing images that are helping us unlock the universe's mysteries.

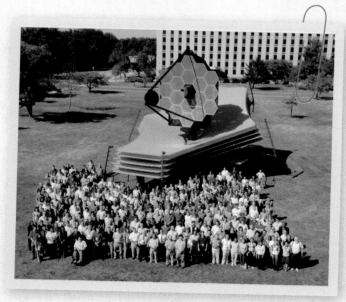

Some of the NASA Webb Telescope team, standing in front of a model of the telescope.

This is how the telescope looked after launch, but before it unfolded.

THE BEST VIEW

The Webb Telescope was designed to give us one of the deepest views of the universe we've ever had. The telescope's enormous mirror allows it to take incredibly detailed images. This gives scientists as much information as possible, helping them figure out what they can see and determine what it means.

The unfolding

To give us a detailed view, the Webb Telescope needed to be big. In fact, at full size it is too big to fit on a rocket, so it had to be folded up. Once launched, it then had to spend a month being unfolded and set up. There were more than 300 steps to go through, and the telescope would have failed if any one step wasn't completed.

The telescope was folded and fueled up before it was attached to a rocket for launch.

How the telescope unfolded

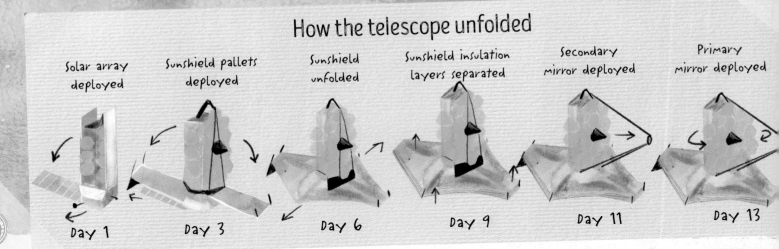

Solar array deployed	Sunshield pallets deployed	Sunshield unfolded	Sunshield insulation layers separated	Secondary mirror deployed	Primary mirror deployed
Day 1	Day 3	Day 6	Day 9	Day 11	Day 13

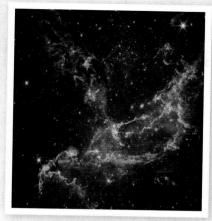

This is a picture taken by the Hubble Telescope, using visible light. It shows NGC 346, a young cluster of stars.

This is the same view, taken by the Webb Telescope, using infrared. We can learn more by investigating the differences.

Different perspectives

The giant golden mirror of the Webb Telescope collects a type of light called infrared, which means it acts a little like a heat vision camera. Infrared is useful because it passes through clouds of dust, which would block visible light. So, using infrared allows us to see things in new ways.

Multi-camera

The Webb Telescope contains four main cameras. Each of these can do different jobs. The Mid-Infrared Instrument (MIRI) looks at types of light that are difficult to see from the ground. It is designed to focus on the light the other cameras on the telescope can't see.

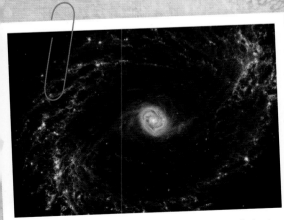

MIRI can see clearly through clouds of dust, which lets us take new views of galaxies, such as this one of NGC 1433.

The Webb Telescope can also look at objects close to home. In its first year of operation it was tasked with taking several pictures of things in our own solar system.

CLOSE-UP PHOTOS

The hot clouds of Jupiter glow brightly in this image. Its moon, Europa, is surprisingly bright when imaged in infrared.

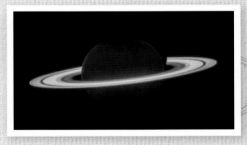

Saturn appears quite dull in infrared—the clouds on its surface stop any heat from escaping, but its rings stand out clearly.

Webb even managed to snap this picture of a comet. The instruments on board detected water coming off the comet.

The Orion Nebula is an enormous cloud of gas and dust that is currently forming thousands of new stars.

DEEP SPACE

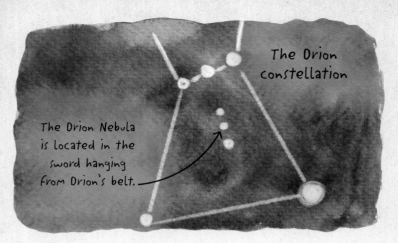

The Orion constellation

The Orion Nebula is located in the sword hanging from Orion's belt.

BIRTH OF A STAR

The universe is full of millions and millions of stars. These enormous balls of fusing gas shine light and heat out into space around them, but where do they come from? These amazing objects begin in giant clouds of gas and dust, called nebulas.

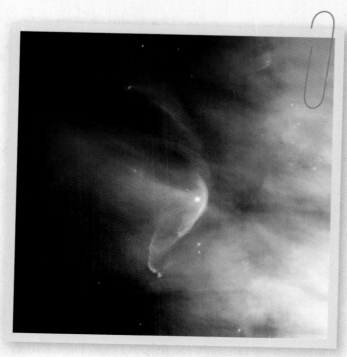

When a new star forms in a nebula, it pushes against the material swirling around it. This creates an effect called a bow shock.

Baby star

Dust cloud

The Carina Nebula is a great example of an old star-forming nebula. As new stars formed, they have carved away at the huge cloud of gas and dust, leaving some interesting shapes.

FIRST FUSION

When the universe began, the main element found in it was hydrogen. Giant gas clouds were slowly pulled together by the force of gravity. Once enough gas is pulled into a small enough space, a reaction called fusion begins and a star is born.

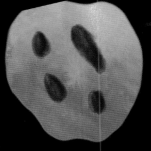

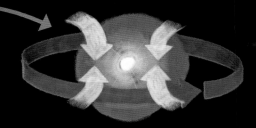

Step 1

Lumps of gas get bigger, causing the middle of them to heat up. This happens because the material is squashed together.

Step 2

As more material is gathered, the pressure and heat increase. The amount of gravity also increases, so even more material gets pulled in. The material also begins to rotate.

Step 3

Eventually, the temperature is high enough to force the atoms of hydrogen together in a fusion reaction. This gives out lots of heat and light energy.

How stars form

To make stars, all you need is gas, gravity, and time. Gravity is a force that causes all material to be attracted to other material. The hydrogen gas in the early universe didn't form evenly—there were lumpy areas with more material. More material means more gravity, so these clumps slowly pulled more gas toward them, making the lumps even bigger.

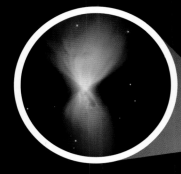

Sometimes the material is pushed away at the poles of the new star. This causes amazing patterns, called bipolar outflows. The Boomerang Nebula (above) is a great example of this.

Step 4

As this energy is released, the star begins to shine and pushes away most of the extra material.

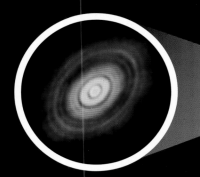

This image of a protoplanetary disk shows bands starting to form around a new star. They will probably become planets.

Step 5

Sometimes, some material remains in a disk around the star. This is called a protoplanetary disk. It can go on to form planets, such as those in our solar system.

Dl Chamaeleontis is a four-star system. This image from the Hubble Space Telescope shows two of these stars, with a cloud of dust swirling around them.

DI Chamaeleontis is part of the Chameleon constellation.

MULTIPLE STAR SYSTEMS

When we think of star systems, we think of planets orbiting around a central star, just like we orbit around the sun. However, the reality can be very different. As astronomers have explored space, they have discovered that many star systems contain more than one star. As many as nine stars have been seen sharing a solar system!

Polaris Aa

Polaris Ab

Polaris, the North Star, is a double star system. We can see its tiny companion in this Hubble image.

SOLAR COUSINS

Stars usually form in groups, in giant clouds of gas and dust called nebulas. Recently, we have discovered that not only do stars form in groups, but they also often form very close together in multiple star systems. These can have two, three, or more stars orbiting around each other, forming complex solar systems.

Optical doubles

The first stars thought to be in multiple systems were "optical doubles." These stars appeared to be close together because of the angle we saw them at from Earth, but they weren't actually linked. Good examples of this are Alcor and Mizar, in the Ursa Major constellation. These two stars look close together, despite being in two separate star systems.

URSA MAJOR

Castor

The more we investigate stars, the more complex systems we find. Castor is in the constellation of Gemini. Castor is part of a six-star system. It consists of three pairs of stars in a complex orbital dance around each other.

Alcor

The stars Alcor and Mizar are positioned in the tail of the constellation Ursa Major.

Mizar

ALCOR AND MIZAR

Surprise stars

Astronomers studying Alcor and Mizar through a telescope discovered that Mizar appeared to be more than one star. Further investigation showed that Mizar was actually four stars in two pairs, orbiting each other over the course of thousands of years. So, Mizar is a multiple star system after all.

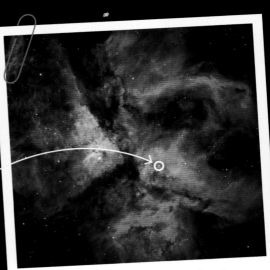

Qz Carinae

The most complex system found so far is QZ Carinae, which has a massive nine stars in a single system.

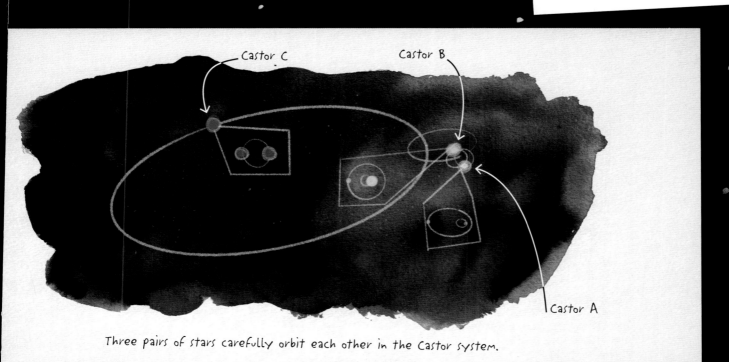

Castor C

Castor B

Castor A

Three pairs of stars carefully orbit each other in the Castor system.

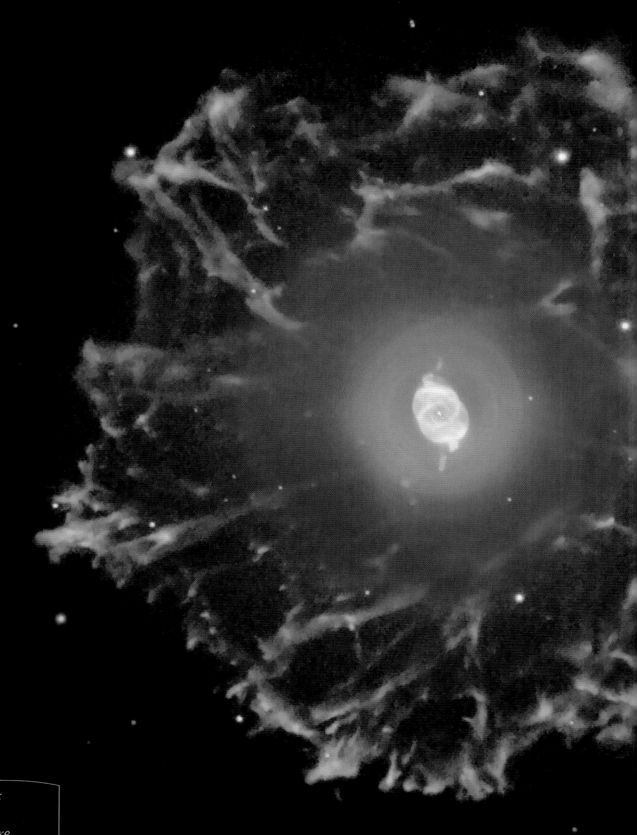

This image shows the Cat's Eye Nebula. You can see where the star's atmosphere has blown away.

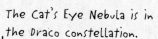

DEATH OF A STAR

What happens to a star at the end of its life depends on the size and mass of the star, but all the possibilities are spectacular. We are going to look at what happens to a star about the same size as our own sun: it expands, shrinks, and blows material out into space, leaving behind a beautiful cloud called a nebula.

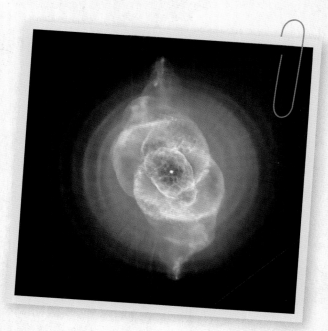

This image shows the central region of the Cat's Eye Nebula. You can see the small white remains of the star at the center, with beautiful patterns of plasma (superhot gas) around it.

BECOMING UNBALANCED

A star is in a constant battle between gravity trying to pull it in, and a force from the energy produced by the star (called radiation pressure) pushing out. As the star runs out of its hydrogen fuel, several events occur that lead to its final fate—to become a small, hot white star called a white dwarf.

AVERAGE-SIZED STAR

As a star runs out of fuel it heats up and expands.

RED GIANT

The red giant collapses in on itself.

COLLAPSED RED GIANT

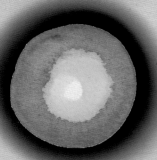

The red giant cools, becoming a planetary nebula.

PLANETARY NEBULA

The core of the star cools, becoming a white dwarf.

WHITE DWARF

This process takes a few billion years.

Becoming a giant

When the star is nearly out of fuel, the outward pressure drops and gravity pulls the star in. As this happens, the star gets very hot and is able to use the last of its fuel. It rapidly grows and cools, becoming a red giant star.

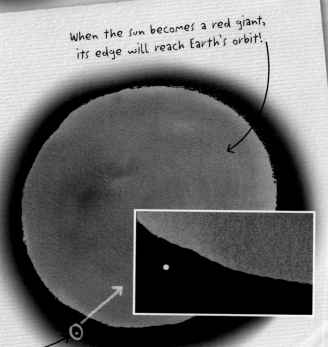

When the sun becomes a red giant, its edge will reach Earth's orbit!

For comparison, this white dot is the sun at its current size.

Big blowout

Becoming a red giant is a star's last gasp. Eventually, it uses up all its fuel and collapses in again. This causes a shockwave and the star blows most of its gases out into space, forming a giant cloud of hot gas called a planetary nebula.

This Hubble Telescope image of the Butterfly Nebula shows how the layers of this star's atmosphere have been blown out into space.

White dwarf star

At the center of the nebula lies the remains of the star—its core. This is very small and very hot and, so, it shines white, as a white dwarf. Over a very long time this star will cool and eventually fade away.

For comparison, this is the size of the sun now, compared to what it will become (right).

This is what will happen to our own star, the sun. But don't worry, this won't happen for at least another 4.5 billion years (longer than Earth has existed so far)!

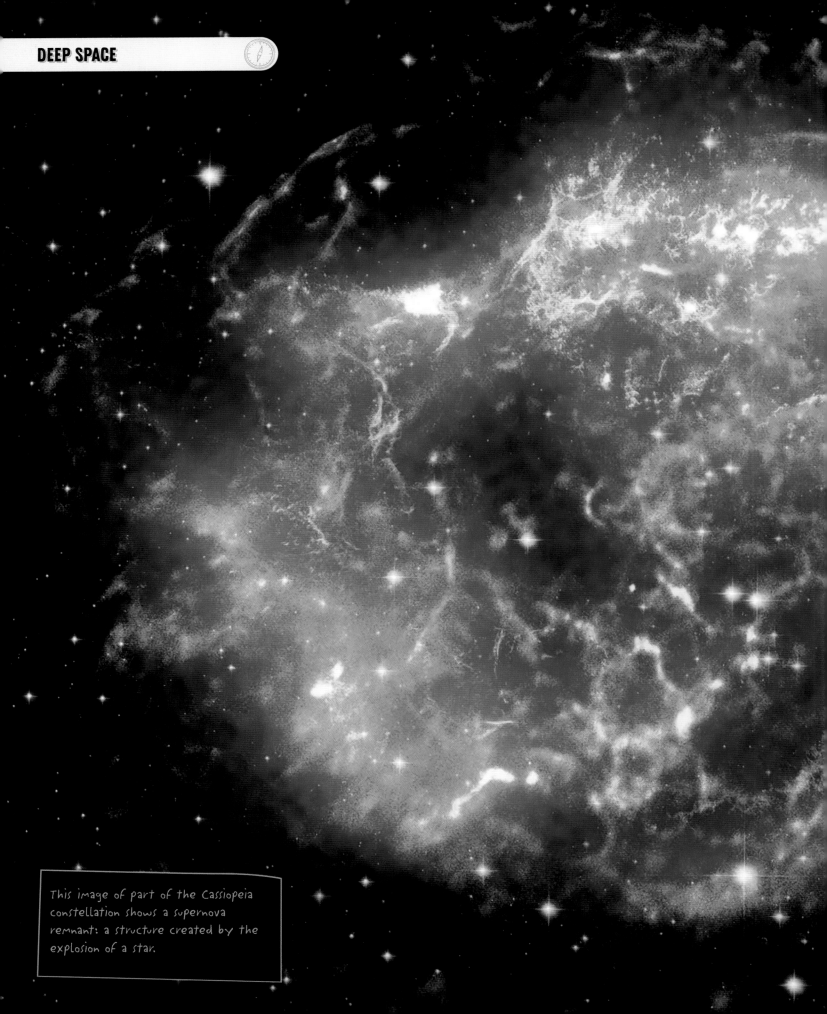

This image of part of the Cassiopeia constellation shows a supernova remnant: a structure created by the explosion of a star.

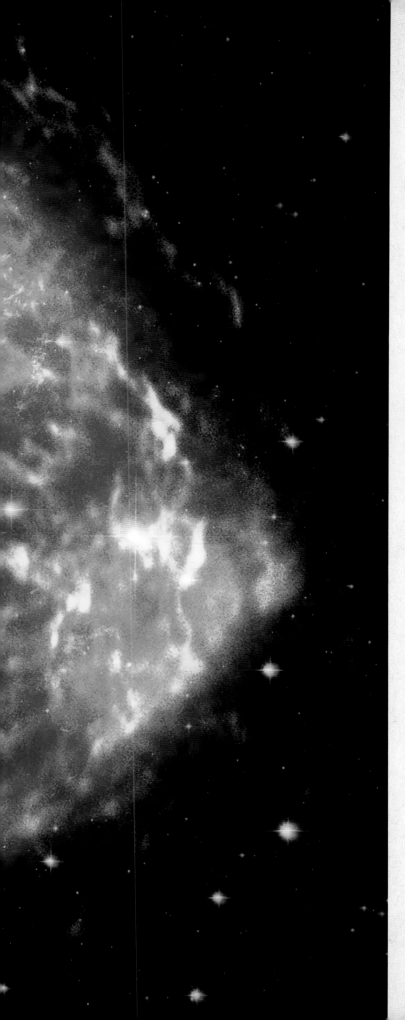

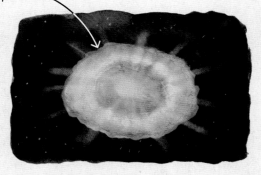

An artist's impression of a supernova.

SUPERNOVAS

Supermassive stars are much bigger than our sun. They burn fast and die young. Once a supermassive star reaches the end of its life, it exits in a spectacular explosion called a supernova. Supernovas are the brightest events in our universe.

NASA's Swift space observatory constantly searches for supernovas to observe.

AMAZING EXPLOSIONS

When a giant star reaches the end of its life, the colossal force of gravity pulling on it triggers a giant shockwave, called a supernova.

Early observations

The first recording of a supernova was made by Chinese astronomers in 185 CE. In 1604, astronomer Johannes Kepler spotted a bright new star in the constellation Ophiuchus that was actually a supernova. Telescopes can still see the remains of this supernova today.

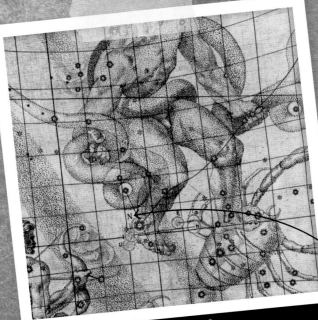

Kepler's supernova was seen as a short-lived bright star. He noted it on his constellation map with the letter "N."

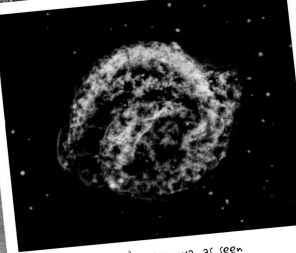

Kepler's supernova, as seen by telescopes today.

SIGNIFICANT SUPERNOVAS

The first

SN 185 was the first supernova humans recorded, spotted by Chinese astronomers in 185 CE. Today, just the supernova remnant, RCW 86 (left), remains.

NASA's NuSTAR telescope is giving scientists new information about what happens during a supernova.

Hunting for supernovas

Supernovas give out huge amounts of energy, including X-rays and Gamma rays. Scientists use telescopes to scan the skies, looking for these giant explosions. When the start of an explosion is seen, other telescopes are ordered to look at it, collecting as much information as possible.

The closest

Also one of the brightest ever seen, SN1054 was documented in the thirtheenth century. Today, the Crab Nebula (right) remains in its place.

The youngest

SN 2023ixf is one of the youngest supernovas we know of. It was spotted in the Pinwheel Galaxy in 2023 as a bright white dot in one of the galaxy's arms.

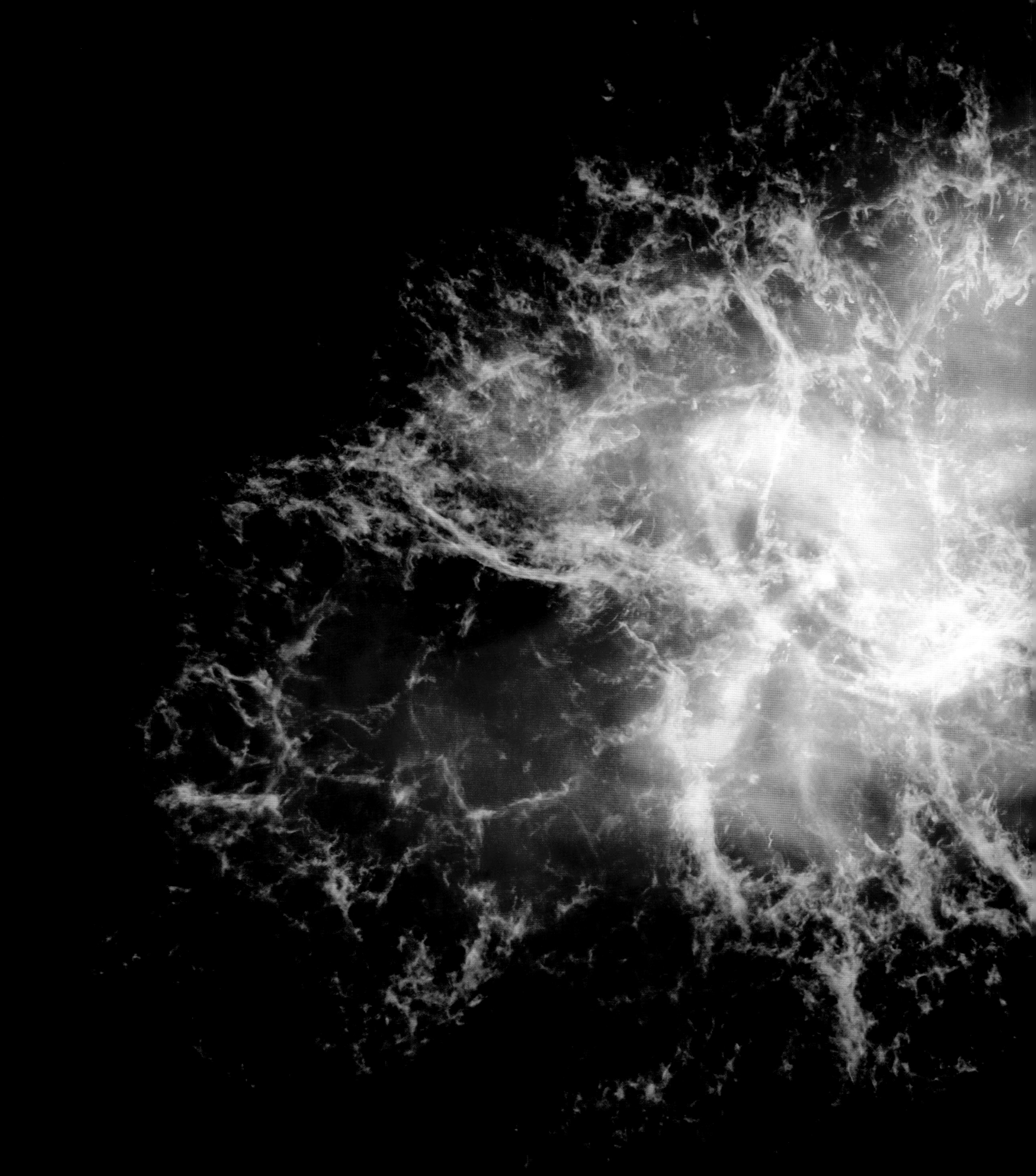

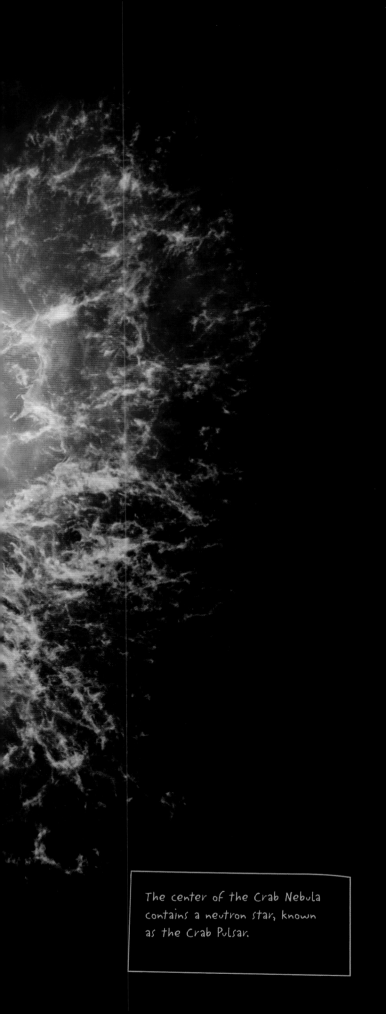

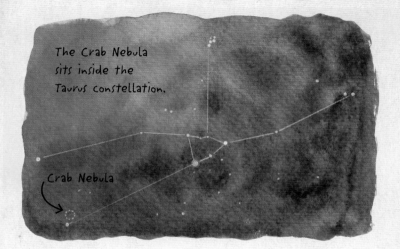

The Crab Nebula sits inside the Taurus constellation.

Crab Nebula

NEUTRON STARS AND BLACK HOLES

When the biggest stars run out of fuel, the result are explosive. These colossal supernovas are so powerful that they test the limits of the laws of physics. However, the objects that come after a supernova are perhaps even more amazing and unique.

A supermassive black hole

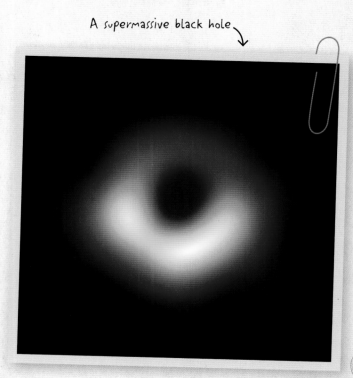

The center of the Crab Nebula contains a neutron star, known as the Crab Pulsar.

GHOSTS OF GIANT STARS

Supernovas are mammoth explosions that blow away the outer layer of the star, while the remaining matter collapses in on itself. This remaining core can form beautiful objects called neutron stars. However, the biggest stars leave behind the strangest and most mysterious objects in the universe—black holes.

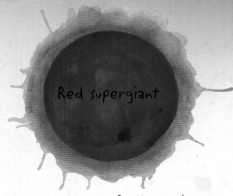

Red supergiant

Really massive stars eventually run out of fuel.

Supernova

This causes the outler layers of the stars to explode, leaving behind a core.

Black hole

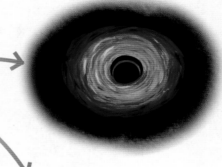

If the core is more than 3 times as massive as the sun, it collapses, forming a black hole.

Neutron star

If the core is 1.5 to 3 times the size of the sun, it becomes a neutron star.

Neutron stars

Although they are small, neutron stars contain a lot of material. To turn Earth into a similar object, the entire planet would need to be squashed down to the size of a tennis court. Neutron stars spin incredibly fast—some of them rotate thousands of times a minute.

This image shows the Crab Pulsar. A pulsar is a fast-spinning neutron star. The rainbow ripples here are caused by rapid spinning.

Black holes

A huge amount of energy is needed to create a black hole. This is why only the biggest stars, and therefore the biggest supernovas, produce them. Black holes have a huge amount of gravity, because they contain so much material.

Jet of high-energy radiation

The black sphere in the center is the black hole itself.

Accretion disk

Powerful gravity

Black holes are created when the star's core is extremely squashed, equivalent to Earth being squeezed to the size of a quarter. This causes gravity to be so strong in a black hole that not even light can escape.

SPOTTING BLACK HOLES

Accretion disks

It is very difficult to see black holes, since they can't glow or reflect light. Luckily, many black holes are surrounded by huge glowing disks, called accretion disks. These disks are made of material that is sucked into the black hole. Gravity causes the material to rub together and glow.

Cosmic lens

The gravity of black holes can be so strong that they bend light as it travels through space. Observing this bending of light helps astronomers find black holes. It also allows them to get a different view of other objects in space. This is called gravitational lensing.

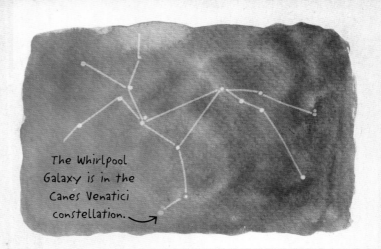

The Whirlpool Galaxy is in the Canes Venatici constellation. →

GALAXIES

Galaxies are huge collections of hundreds of billions of stars, their planets and moons, gases and dust, held together by gravity in a dance around a central point. Galaxies also contain a mysterious material called dark matter, which was only discovered by studying how galaxies rotate!

Some galaxies look very different when viewed from the side. The below image shows the side of spiral galaxy NGC 1055.

PICTURE PERFECT

Galaxies are one of the most photographed
objects in space. Some, such as our galaxy,
the Milky Way, have beautiful spiral arms of
stars wrapped around them. Others look
more like squashed balls of stars.

Scientists now believe
that a black hole lies
at the heart of
almost every galaxy.

Spiral galaxies

These have a central bulge, with spiral
arms of stars fanning out from it.

Galaxy shapes

Galaxies are organized into three main
categories based on their shape.

Elliptical galaxies

These collections of stars are round
and roughly egg-shaped.

Viewing the Milky Way

We live inside the Orion arm of the Milky Way Galaxy. At the right time of year, on really clear nights, the other arms of our galaxy can sometimes be seen. They appear as milky bands of stars stretching across the night sky.

This image of the Phantom Galaxy was taken by the James Webb Space Telescope. It captures different wavelengths to reveal otherwise hidden objects.

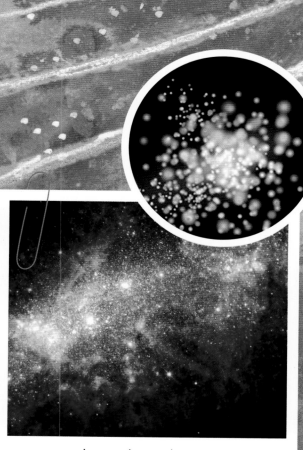

Irregular galaxies

There is no clear structure to these collections of stars.

Mysterious matter

Most galaxies rotate around a black hole. The way they rotate suggests that there is a lot more material in them than what we can see. We call this invisible material dark matter, and we still have a lot to learn about it.

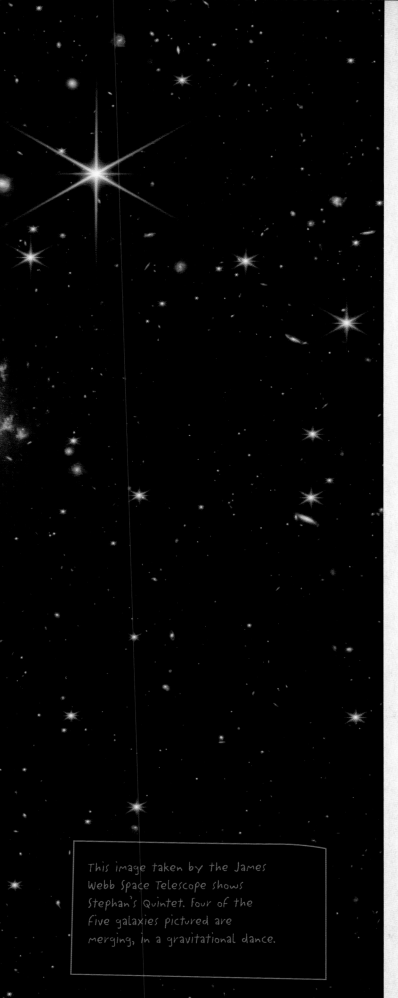

This image taken by the James Webb Space Telescope shows Stephan's Quintet. Four of the five galaxies pictured are merging, in a gravitational dance.

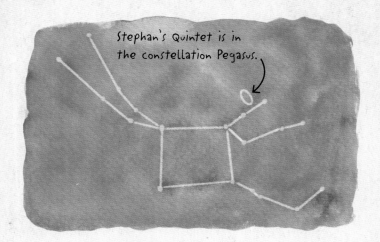

Stephan's Quintet is in the constellation Pegasus.

COSMIC COLLISIONS

Galaxies, such as our Milky Way, are collections of hundreds of billions of stars and planets held together by gravity. Most galaxies have their own neighborhood in space, but sometimes they may move toward each other and collide.

The Hubble Space Telescope has snapped many images of colliding galaxies over the years, such as the Antennae Galaxies, above.

GRAVITY'S PULL

Galaxies are enormous! With so much stuff in them, they have a lot of gravity. If two galaxies are close to each other, they will pull each other in, swirling around until eventually they merge into one. So, what does this mean for us?

Andromeda alert

Our Milky Way is on a collision course with the Andromeda Galaxy. The galaxies are moving toward each other at more than 60 miles (100 km) per second! But don't panic— they won't merge for another 4 billion years.

Milky Way

The Milky Way is currently 2.5 million light-years away from the Andromeda Galaxy.

The two galaxies are being drawn together because they each have a huge gravitational pull.

Andromeda

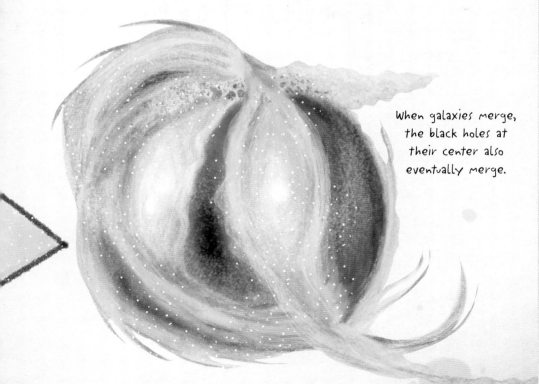

This image of galaxies merging shows them pulling material from each other as they get closer.

Big mergers

Collisions between galaxies are more of a merge than a crash. The stars don't collide with each other, but the galaxies pull material from each other in a gravity dance, which can trigger the formation of new stars.

When galaxies merge, the black holes at their center also eventually merge.

Milkomeda
IN 4 BILLION YEARS

OTHER COLLIDING GALAXIES

Sprial galaxy NGC 4911 is in the Coma Cluster, an area of space home to almost 1,000 galaxies. NGC 4911 is being pulled apart by its many neighbors.

UGC 1810, the upper galaxy, will be devouring Arp 273, the lower galaxy, over the next billion years.

This pair, called NGC 6240, is extra-bright. The two galaxies are just about to merge as one, creating a lot of energy.

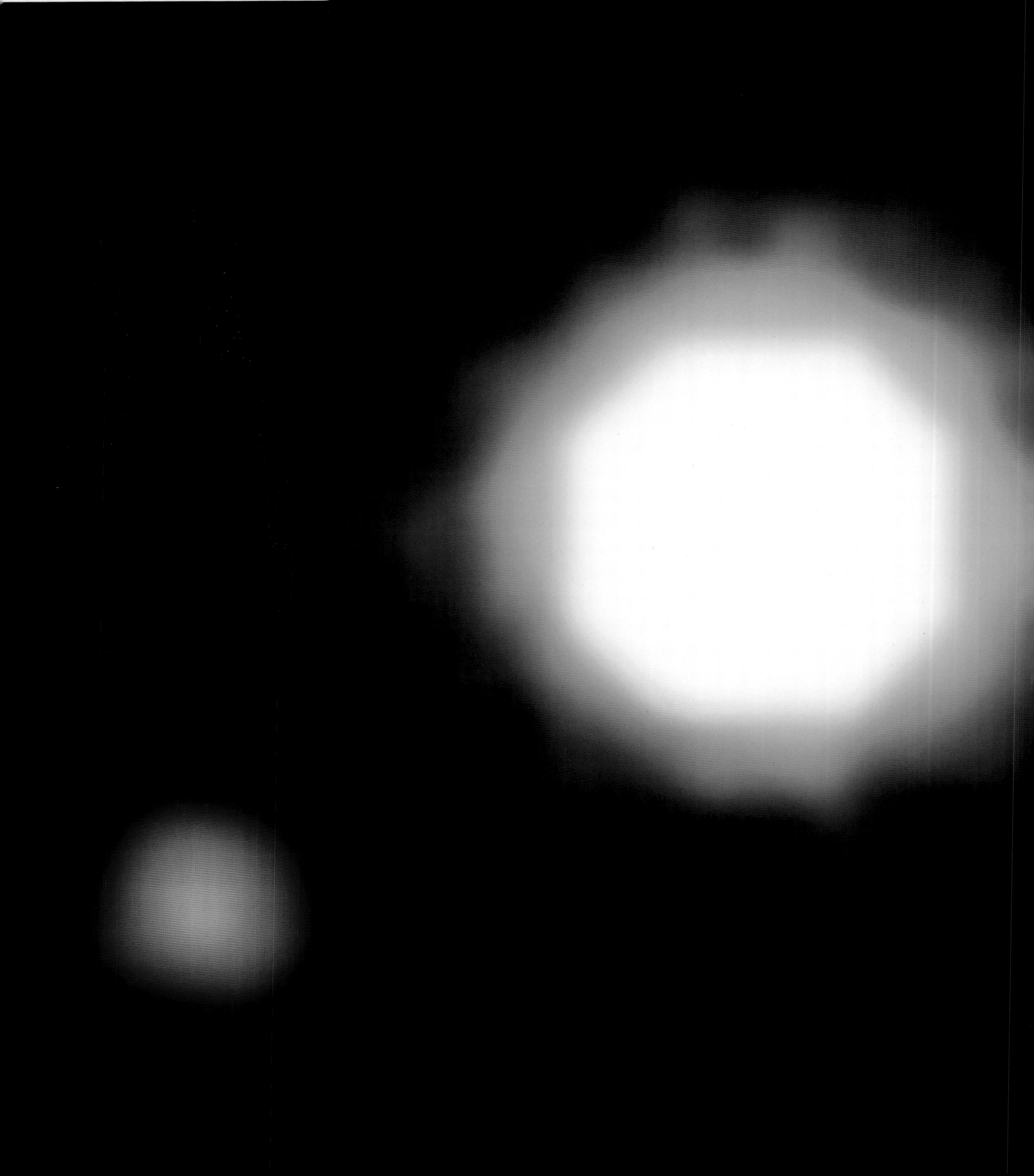

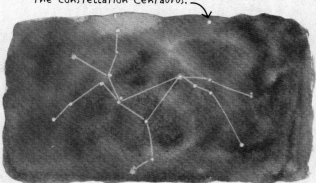

The planet 2M1207b is located in the constellation Centaurus.

EXOPLANETS

Most of the planets in our solar system were discovered thousands of years ago, but it was only recently that astronomers imagined that other stars might have worlds orbiting around them. As scientists have been able to look farther into space, they have discovered that the universe is full of these exoplanets.

This is the very first picture of a planet orbiting around a star other than our sun! The planet is called 2M1207b.

This is an artist's impression of 2M1207b. It is a gas giant about fives times as massive as Jupiter, making it a "super-Jupiter."

DISTANT WORLDS

An exoplanet is a planet that orbits a star other than our sun. Astronomers first found proof they existed in 1992. Since then, more than 5,000 exoplanets have been discovered, and this number is always growing.

Giant discoveries

Because they're so far away, bigger exoplanets are easier find. This means that early discoveries were usually gas giants. They could be found by looking for a "wobble" in the star that they orbit, caused by the exoplanet's gravity.

Exoplanet orbit

Exoplanet

Star

Light from an object moving toward us is bluer, because it's squashed.

Wobble

Light from an object moving away from us is more red, because it's stretched.

Earth

As a large planet orbits a star, it causes the star to wobble. If we measure the light from a star, we can detect this wobble. It can even tell us the exoplanet's size.

The Doppler effect

If a car drives past with sirens on, the change of pitch is the sound waves being squashed (as it gets closer) and stretched (as it moves away). This is called the Doppler effect, and it explains why light from wobbling stars appears more blue (squashed) or red (stretched).

If the car is not moving, the sound waves are not stretched.

As the car moves closer, the waves are squashed.

As the car moves away, the waves are stretched.

Smaller discoveries

Small planets don't wobble their stars enough to be detected. So, another great way to find planets is to find stars that have changes in their brightness. As planets move between their parent star and us, they block a tiny amount of light. We can use this to figure out how big the exoplanet is, and how long it takes to orbit.

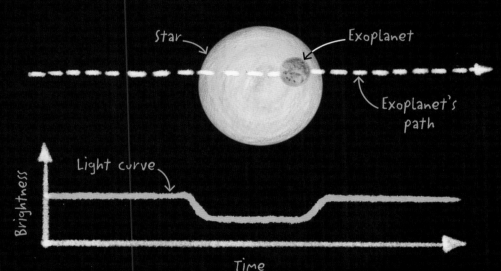

Star

Exoplanet

Exoplanet's path

Light curve

Brightness

Time

This graph shows a dip in the brightness of this star. As a result, scientists know an exoplanet has moved across it.

Unique planets

Astronomers have discovered some amazing exoplanets. In 2011, Kepler-10b was discovered: a tiny rocky planet so close to its star that its surface is likely one giant lava lake. Another planet, called 55 Cancri, is so hot and heavy that scientists think it's made almost entirely of diamond!

Kepler-10b

55 Cancri

Multiple Earths

One of the most amazing star systems we have found is the Trappist-1 star system, which contains seven planets. The star is much smaller than our sun, so the whole system is much smaller. Despite this, there could be at least two planets very similar to Earth.

Every 15 years or so, these mysterious smudges occur on Saturn's rings, and astronomers have no idea why.

SPACE MYSTERIES

We are getting very good at understanding and explaining what we see in the images that space telescopes and probes send back to us. However, we do find things that we struggle to explain. Scientists have figured out some things, but others are still a mystery!

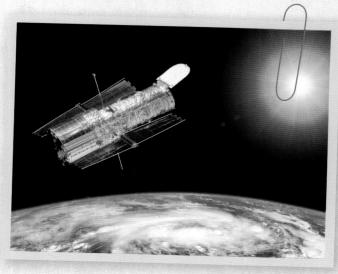

The image on the left (of Saturn's rings) was taken by the Hubble Space Telescope.

WHAT, WHY, AND HOW?

Scientists love to be surprised, and space has a lot of surprising images for them. A mysterious space image lets astronomers play detective to try and understand what is going on, and can improve our understanding of science at the same time! But these pictures can also fire the imagination, and some people come up with wild theories to explain the sights.

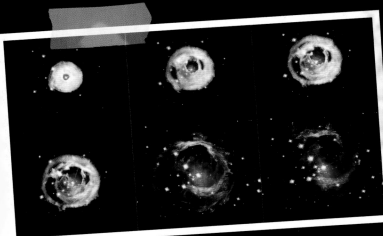

Light pulsed through the clouds of dust and gas surrounding V838 Monocerotis, making it look like the cloud was expanding.

V838 Monocerotis

Pulsing Monocerotis

In 2002, V838 Monocerotis, a previously unremarkable star, suddenly brightened, becoming a million times brighter than our sun. The light traveled through the ancient clouds of dust and gas around the star, lighting it up and making it look as though it was expanding. Scientists believe this may have been caused by two stars merging together—but they are still not certain.

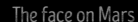

The face on Mars

In 1976, the Viking 1 orbiter sent back an image of the surface of Mars that shocked scientists: it appeared to show a face! Some people suggested that this had been built by an ancient Martian civilization, but scientists suspected that it was a trick of the light. Newer images show that it was caused by shadows.

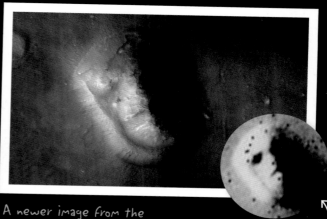

A newer image from the Mars Global Surveyor, with better resolution and reduced shadows.

Original image

Tabby's Star

Variable stars are stars that get brighter and dimmer over time, usually with a fixed pattern. Tabby's Star seems to get brighter and dimmer at random, and scientists are still trying to confirm why. The most likely explanation is that it is surrounded by a "lumpy" ring of gas, which blocks different amounts of light at different times.

GLOSSARY

asteroid
A small, lumpy object in the solar system, usually made of either rock or metals.

asteroid belt
A huge, ring-shaped region of the solar system, located between the planets Mars and Jupiter, which contains many asteroids (and the dwarf planet Ceres).

atmosphere
The layer of gases that surrounds an object, such as a planet or moon.

auroras
Glowing bands of light that appear in the atmosphere above the polar regions of a planet or moon. On Earth, in the northern hemisphere they are called the aurora borealis, while in the southern hemisphere they are known as the aurora australis.

Big Bang
The name given to the event that marked the birth of the universe. It is thought the universe was incredibly hot and must have quickly expanded in size from a single, small point.

black hole
A very dense, ball-shaped region of space, caused by a collapsed star. Light cannot travel fast enough to escape the powerful gravitational pull of a black hole, so these mysterious objects are almost completely black.

comet
An icy object in the solar system that warms and begins to release gases as it approaches the sun.

constellation
A group of stars that forms a pattern, often named after a mythological figure.

core
The innermost layer of a planet or moon. It can be solid or liquid.

crater
A pit in the surface of a planet, moon, or other solid space object. Craters are formed when asteroids, comets, and other smaller space rocks crash into a surface.

dark matter
Mysterious material that does not absorb, reflect, or emit light.

dense
Containing a lot of matter in a small space.

dwarf planet
A round object in space that orbits the sun, but is not a moon. Smaller than a planet, it does not have the size to clear its orbit from objects.

eclipse
When one object in space moves in front of another and blocks light from reaching an observer.

electromagnetic spectrum
The range of radiation in the universe, organized by wavelength. Humans are only able to see visible light, but telescopes can detect other wavelengths on the spectrum.

exoplanet
A planet that orbits another star outside our own solar system. There are likely billions of these worlds in our galaxy.

galaxy
A huge gathering of thousands, millions, or sometimes even billions of stars that swirl together through the universe.

galaxy cluster
A collection of multiple galaxies that exist in a relatively close group.

gas giant
A large planet with low density, usually made mainly of hydrogen and helium. In our solar system, Jupiter, Saturn, Uranus, and Neptune are gas giants.

gravity
The force of attraction that exists between all matter. The larger the mass of an object, the greater its gravitational pull.

heliosphere
The region surrounding our sun and the solar system that is filled with solar wind. Beyond the heliosphere is interstellar space (space between stars).

helium
The second most-common chemical element in the universe, after hydrogen.

hydrogen
A chemical element that is found all over the cosmos. Most stars are mainly made of hydrogen.

infrared
A wavelength that is greater than the red end of the visible light spectrum, but shorter than microwaves.

Kuiper belt
A large expanse of the solar system beyond the orbit of the planet Neptune that contains many small, frozen bodies. Pluto orbits the sun within the Kuiper belt region.

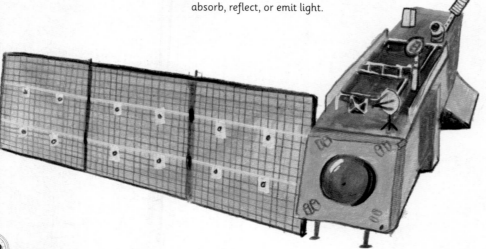

light-year

The distance traveled by a beam of light in one Earth year. Light-years are used as a way to describe the huge distances to and between faraway objects in the universe, such as stars and galaxies.

magnetic field

An area around a planet or moon that shields it from solar wind.

mantle

The inner layer of a planet that surrounds the core.

meteor

A small object from outer space that enters Earth's atmosphere, becoming bright and appearing as a streak of light.

meteorite

A space rock, or a fragment of a space rock, that has made it through Earth's atmosphere to land on the surface of our planet.

meteoroid

A small body moving in the solar system that would become a meteor if it entered Earth's atmosphere.

microbes

A tiny living thing that is too small to be seen with the naked eye.

microwave

A wavelength that is shorter than radio waves, but larger than infrared.

Milky Way

The name of our home galaxy. We see the Milky Way from the inside, as our sun is one of the 200–400 billion stars that calls the Milky Way home.

moon

The name given to the natural objects—big and small—that orbit around the various worlds, and other objects, in our solar system and beyond.

nebula

A cloud of gas and dust floating in space.

neutron star

The collapsed core of a massive star left after a supernova.

nuclear fusion

The reaction that powers the sun and other stars.

Oort cloud

A huge sphere of icy, cometlike objects that is thought to surround the solar system.

orbit

The path one object takes around another—such as Earth's path around the sun, a comet's journey through the solar system, or even the route taken by one galaxy whirling around another.

planet

Any one of the eight main worlds in our solar system: Mercury, Venus, Earth, Mars, Jupiter, Saturn, Uranus, and Neptune. There are planets around other stars too— see "exoplanet."

plasma

A very hot gas that has a lot more energy than the other three states of matter (solids, liquids, and gases).

pulsar

A rapidly rotating neutron star.

red shift

The increase in wavelength of light from objects that are moving away from us

rings

Grains, clumps, or large chunks of material, often icy, that orbit around an object in space.

satellite

Usually refers to the human-made objects that travel around Earth, or other bodies in the solar system. Sometimes astronomers refer to moons as the natural satellites of planets.

solar system

The varied collection of objects— including planets, moons, asteroids, and comets—that orbit the sun.

solar wind

Charged particles released by the sun across the solar system.

space junk

Human-made debris that is no longer in use, but still orbits Earth.

space station

A human-made satellite used as a long-term base for space exploration.

star

An enormous ball of plasma that shines because of a reaction called nuclear fusion. Eventually, the reactions slow down and stop when the star dies.

star system

A small number of stars that orbit each other, bound by gravity.

supernova

An extremely powerful explosion created by a large, dying star.

universe

All of space and everything it contains.

INDEX

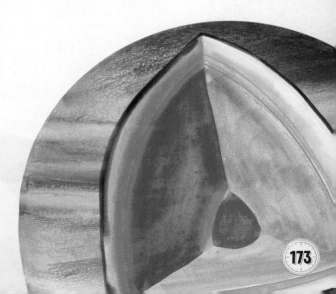

ACKNOWLEDGMENTS

DK would like to thank: Polly Goodman for proofreading and Helen Peters for the index.

The publisher would like to thank the following for their kind permission to reproduce their photographs:

(Key: a=above; b=below/bottom; c=center; f=far; l=left; r=right; t=top)

1-176 **Dreamstime.com:** Daboost. 2-3 **ESA / Hubble:** NASA, R. Cohen. 8-9 **NASA:** NOAA / GSFC / Suomi NPP / VIIRS / Norman Kuring. 9 **NASA:** (br). 10-11 **NASA.** 10 **NASA:** (bc). 11 **ESA:** Kari (tc). **NASA:** JSC (cr). 12-13 **Getty Images / iStock:** TZU-HAN-YU. 15 **ESA:** NASA–T. Pesquet (br). **NASA:** SDO (cra). 16-17 **NASA:** Joel Kowsky. 17 **NASA:** (br). 18 **123RF.com:** picsfive (b). **Dreamstime.com:** Robyn Mackenzie / Robynmac (Tape). 19 **123RF.com:** picsfive (r). **Alamy Stock Photo:** Planetpix (cb); PR images (crb). **NASA:** (tl, tr). **Virgin Galactic:** (cr). 20-21 **ESA:** NASA / JPL-Caltech. 21 **Dreamstime.com:** Jeerawat Pokeeree (crb). 22 **Science Photo Library:** Mark Williamson (b). 23 **123RF.com:** picsfive (cl). **Dreamstime.com:** Robyn Mackenzie / Robynmac (cla). **Japan Aerospace Exploration Agency (JAXA):** (cra). **Science Photo Library:** Nicolle R. Fuller (br). 24-25 **NASA.** 25 **NASA:** (br). 26 **Dreamstime.com:** Robyn Mackenzie / Robynmac (clb). **NASA:** (r, br). 26-27 **123RF.com:** picsfive (b). 27 **123RF.com:** picsfive (t). **Dreamstime.com:** Robyn Mackenzie / Robynmac (tl, tc). **NASA:** (cla, cr, cb, bl, bc). 28-29 **NASA.** 29 **Alamy Stock Photo:** IanDagnall Computing (br). 30 **123RF.com:** picsfive (br). **NASA:** (tr). 31 **Alamy Stock Photo:** Pictorial Press Ltd (tl); Misha Japaridze / Associated Press (crb). **Dreamstime.com:** Ilyach (b). **NASA:** (clb). 32-33 **Science Photo Library:** Mikkel Juul Jensen. 33 **ESA:** (br). 34 **123RF.com:** picsfive (b). 35 **Alamy Stock Photo:** Stephen Hovington (tl). **NASA:** (bl). 36-37 **Alamy Stock Photo:** Pictorial Press Ltd. 37 **Alamy Stock Photo:** Album (crb). 38 **Dreamstime.com:** Robyn Mackenzie / Robynmac (ca, clb). **NASA:** Dominic Hart (cb). **PLoS ONE:** Lee S-J (2007) Quadrupling Muscle Mass in Mice by Targeting TGF-ß Signaling Pathways. PLoS ONE 2(8): e789. https://doi.org/10.1371/journal.pone.0000789 (cl). 38-39 **123RF.com:** picsfive (b). 39 **Alamy Stock Photo:** NIH / IMAGE POINT FR / BSIP (cl); Science History Images (tr). 40-41 **NASA.** 41 **NASA:** (br). 42-43 **123RF.com:** picsfive (b). 42 **Alamy Stock Photo:** NASA (br). **Dreamstime.com:** Robyn Mackenzie / Robynmac (clb). **NASA:** (c). **Science Photo Library:** NASA (bl). 43 **Alamy Stock Photo:** Photo Researchers / Science History Images (bc). 44-45 **Getty Images:** Wang Zhao / AFP. 45 **NASA:** (br). 46 **Dreamstime.com:** Robyn Mackenzie / Robynmac (cb). **ESA:** NASA (bc). 47 **Alamy Stock Photo:** Stocktrek Images, Inc. (bc). **Dreamstime.com:** Robyn Mackenzie / Robynmac (tc/Tape). **NASA:** (tc); Glenn Benson (cra). 48-49 **Alamy Stock Photo:** Sipa US. 49 **NASA:** JPL-Caltech (crb). 50-51 **123RF.com:** picsfive (b). 50 **Alamy Stock Photo:** Photo Researchers / Science History Images (bc). **Dreamstime.com:** Robyn Mackenzie / Robynmac (clb). 51 **Alamy Stock Photo:** Walter Myers / Stocktrek Images (bc); World History Archive (bl). 52-53 **NASA:** Johns Hopkins University Applied Physics Laboratory / Carnegie Institution of Washington. 53 **Alamy Stock Photo:** NG Images (br). 54 **123RF.com:** picsfive (bl). **Dreamstime.com:** Robyn Mackenzie / Robynmac (cb). **NASA:** JHU APL / CIW (crb). 54-55 **NASA:** Johns Hopkins University Applied Physics Laboratory / Carnegie Institution of Washington (t). 55 **123RF.com:** picsfive (c). **NASA:** (tl). 56-57 **NASA:** JPL-Caltech. 57 **ESO:** Y. Beletsky (crb). 58 **Science Photo Library:** Detlev Van Ravenswaay (cr). 59 **NASA:** JPL (cr). 60-61 **Alamy Stock Photo:** Martin. 61 **Dreamstime.com:** Robyn Mackenzie / Robynmac (cl). **NASA:** JPL-Caltech (crb). 62 **123RF.com:** picsfive (cra, clb). **Dreamstime.com:** Robyn Mackenzie / Robynmac (tc). **ESA:** DLR / FUBerlin / AndreaLuck (cl). **NASA:** JPL-Caltech / MSSS (tr). 62-63 **Alamy Stock Photo:** Geopix (b). 63 **ESA:** DLR / FU Berlin (tc). 64-65 **NASA:** JPL-Caltech / UCLA / MPS / DLR / IDA. 65 **Shutterstock.com:** Kit Leong (br). 66 **123RF.com:** picsfive (bl). **Dreamstime.com:** Robyn Mackenzie / Robynmac (cb). **NASA:** JPL-Caltech / UCLA / MPS / DLR / PSI and NASA / ESA / STScI / UMd (bl/Vesta); JPL-Caltech / UCLA / MPS / DLR / IDA (bc, bc/Vesta captured by Dawn). 67 **ESO:** Vernazza, Marchis et al. / MISTRAL algorithm (ONERA / CNRS) (tr). **NASA:** JPL-Caltech / ASU (br). 68-69 **NASA:** Enhanced image by Kevin M. Gill (CC-BY) based on images provided courtesy of NASA / JPL-Caltech / SwRI / MSSS. 69 **Science Photo Library:** Rev. Ronald Royer (crb). 71 **Dreamstime.com:** Robyn Mackenzie / Robynmac (c/Tape). **NASA:** Enhanced image by Kevin M. Gill (CC-BY) based on images provided courtesy of NASA / JPL-Caltech / SwRI / MSSS (c); JPL / University of Arizona (tr); JPL-Caltech / SwRI / MSSS / Gerald Eichstad / Sean Doran © CC NC SA (cr). 72-73 **NASA:** ESA and Erich Karkoschka (University of Arizona). 73 **Alamy Stock Photo:** Victor Habbick Visions (crb). 74 **NASA:** JPL-Caltech / Space Science Institute (cl, cb). 74-75 **ESA / Hubble:** NASA, A. Simon (Goddard Space Flight Center), M.H. Wong (University of California, Berkeley), and the OPAL Team (t). 75 **NASA:** JPL / STScI (tr); JPL-Caltech / Space Science Institute (c). 76-77 **Alamy Stock Photo:** Igor Filonenko. 77 **NASA:** JPL-Caltech (crb). 79 **123RF.com:** picsfive (t). **Dreamstime.com:** Ilyach (b). **NASA:** ESA and Erich Karkoschka, University of Arizona (bl). 80-81 **Alamy Stock Photo:** Worldspec / NASA. 81 **NASA:** JPL (crb). 82 **Dreamstime.com:** Robyn Mackenzie / Robynmac (bc/Tape). **ESO:** P. Weilbacher (AIP) (cra). **NASA:** ESA, CSA, STScI (bc); JPL (clb). 83 **123RF.com:** picsfive (t/paper, r). **NASA:** JPL / USGS (tr); JPL (crb). 84-85 **Science Photo Library:** Juan Carlos Casado (Starryearth.com). 85 **Alamy Stock Photo:** Photo Researchers / Science History Images (crb). 86 **Shutterstock.com:** Cessna152. 87 **123RF.com:** picsfive (r). **Alamy Stock Photo:** ESA / Rosetta / Philae / CIVA / Sipa USA (tl); NASA Image Collection (crb). **ESA:** (cr). **NASA:** (cra). 88-89 **Alamy Stock Photo:** NASA Image Collection. 89 **Alamy Stock Photo:** Christophe Coat (cb). **NASA:** Johns Hopkins University Applied Physics Laboratory / Southwest Research Institute (cb/Pluto); NASA Visualization Technology Applications And Development (VTAD) (crb, crb/Makemake); JPL-Caltech / UCLA / MPS / DLR / IDA (fcrb). 90 **NASA:** Johns Hopkins University Applied Physics Laboratory / Southwest Research Institute (c); JPL-Caltech / UCLA / MPS / DLR / IDA (tr). 90-91 **NASA:** Johns Hopkins University Applied Physics Laboratory / Southwest Research Institute (b). 91 **Alamy Stock Photo:** NASA Image Collection (c). **Dreamstime.com:** Robyn Mackenzie / Robynmac (tl). 92-93 **Alamy Stock Photo:** Damian Peach / Galaxy Picture Library. 93 **Alamy Stock Photo:** John White Photos (crb). 95 **ESO:** M. Kornmesser (bc). 96-97 **Alamy Stock Photo:** Geopix. 97 **Science Photo Library:** NASA / SDO / LMSAL (crb). 98 **NASA:** ESA / SOHO (cl). 99 **123RF.com:** picsfive (b). **NASA:** Aubrey Gemignani (tl). 100-101 **NASA.** 101 **Shutterstock.com:** Claudio Caridi (crb). 102 **Dreamstime.com:** Robyn Mackenzie / Robynmac (c). **NASA:** JPL-Caltech / SwRI / MSSS / Kevin M. Gill (tl). 103 **123RF.com:** picsfive (b). **NASA:** Johns Hopkins University Applied Physics Laboratory / Southwest

Research Institute (c); JPL / University of Arizona (cla). **104-105 Alamy Stock Photo:** NASA Image Collection. **105 NASA:** JPL-Caltech / Space Science Institute (crb). **106 123RF.com:** picsfive (crb). **Dreamstime.com:** Robyn Mackenzie / Robynmac (bc, crb/Tape). **NASA:** ESA, and A. Simon (Goddard Space Flight Center); (cb); JPL-Caltech / Space Science Institute / Hampton University (bl). **107 Dreamstime.com:** Robyn Mackenzie / Robynmac (cra). **ESA:** DLR / FU Berlin (cr). **NASA:** JPL-Caltech (cla). **108-109 Alamy Stock Photo:** NASA Image Collection. **109 Alamy Stock Photo:** World History Archive (crb). **110 Dreamstime.com:** Robyn Mackenzie / Robynmac (ca, clb). **NASA:** Orbital ATK (bc). **Shutterstock.com:** Astor57 (cl). **110-111 123RF.com:** picsfive (b). **Dreamstime.com:** Standret. **111 123RF.com:** picsfive (t). **Alamy Stock Photo:** Photo Researchers / Science History Images (br). **ESA:** S. Corvaja (bl). **NASA:** IMAX (c). **Shutterstock. com:** Saad Qamar (cr). **112-113 Science Photo Library:** Eckhard Slawik. **114-115 Dreamstime.com. 115 123RF.com:** picsfive (r). **Dreamstime. com:** Robyn Mackenzie / Robynmac (cla, cb). **Science Photo Library:** John Chumack (crb); Jeff Dai (cl); Gerard Lodriguss (cr). **116-117 NASA:** Bill Ingalls. **117 Science Photo Library:** Jeff Dai (crb). **118 123RF.com:** picsfive (tr). **Dreamstime.com:** Robyn Mackenzie / Robynmac (c). **NASA:** JPL-Caltech (cr). **119 123RF.com:** picsfive; solarseven (tc). **Alamy Stock Photo:** John Cancalosi (ca/Seymchan Meteorite); Susan E. Degginger (cla, fcla); myLAM (ca); Natural History Museum, London (cra). **Dreamstime. com:** Robyn Mackenzie / Robynmac (tl, crb). Randy L. Korotev (cb). **120-121 NASA:** ESA, CSA, and STScI. **121 NASA:** (crb). **122-123 123RF.com:** picsfive (b). **123 ESO:** ALMA (ESO / NAOJ / NRAO) / E. OGorman / P. Kervella (cla). **124-125 Shutterstock.com:** cometa geo. **125 Shutterstock.com:** cometa geo (crb). **126 S. Fatigoni et al. (2021):** (cb). **Dreamstime.com:** Robyn Mackenzie / Robynmac (cb/Tape). **Science Photo Library:** JPL-Caltech / D. Block (Anglo American Cosmic Dust Lab, Sa) / NASA (br); Max-Planck-Institut Fur Radioastronomie (clb). **127 Dreamstime.com:** Robyn Mackenzie / Robynmac (cr). **Science Photo Library:** NASA / Swift / Stefan Immler (Gsfc) And Erin Grand (Umcp) (bc); Smithsonian Institution (crb). **Shutterstock.com:** NASA images (clb). **128-129 NASA:** Desiree Stover. **129 NASA:** GSFC (br). **130 123RF.com:** picsfive (b). **Dreamstime.com:** Robyn Mackenzie / Robynmac (fbl, crb). **Science Photo Library:** European Space Agency / CNES / Arianespace (cr). **131 123RF.com:** picsfive (r). **ESA:** NASA / CSA / STScI (cra); NASA, CSA, STScI, M. Tiscareno (SETI Institute), M. Hedman (University of Idaho), M. El Moutamid (Cornell University), M. Showalter (SETI Institute), L. Fletcher (University of Leicester), H. Hammel (AURA), J. DePasquale (STScI) (cr). **NASA:** ESA, A. James (STScI) (tl); ESA, CSA, STScI, A. Pagan (STScI) (tc); ESA, CSA, and J. Lee (NOIRLab), A. Pagan (STScI) (clb); ESA, CSA, M. Kelley (University of Maryland), H. Hsieh (Planetary Science Institute), A. Pagan (STScI) (crb). **132-133 ESA / Hubble:** NASA, M. Robberto (Space Telescope Science Institute / ESA) and the Hubble Space Telescope Orion Treasury Project Team. **133 NASA:** (crb). **134 ESO:** ALMA (NAOJ / NRAO). NASA and The Hubble Heritage Team (AURA/STScI): NASA, ESA, Mario Livio (STScI), Hubble 20th Anniversary Team (STScI) (clb). **135 ESO:** (clb). **NASA:** ESA and The Hubble Heritage Team (STScI / AURA) (c). **136-137 Alamy Stock Photo:** NG Images. **137 NASA:** ESA, N. Evans (Harvard-Smithsonian CfA), and H. Bond (STScI) (crb). **138 123RF.com:** picsfive (tr/paper). **Dreamstime.com:** Robyn Mackenzie / Robynmac (tr). **139 Alamy Stock Photo:** Historic Collection (cr). **Science Photo Library:** John Sanford (tl). **140-141 Alamy Stock Photo:** NASA Image Collection. **141 NASA:** ESA, HEIC, and The Hubble Heritage Team (STScI / AURA) (crb). **143 NASA:** ESA and the Hubble SM4 ERO Team (tr). **144-145 NASA:** CXC / SAO, IXPE: NASA / MSFC / J. Vink et al.; Optical: NASA / STScI. **145 Science Photo Library:** NASA (crb). **146 Alamy Stock Photo:** World History Archive (cl). Dreamstime.com: Robyn Mackenzie / Robynmac (cla, cb). **NASA:** CXC / NCSU / M.Burkey et al; Optical: DSS (clb); CXC / SAO &Amp; ESA; Infrared: NASA / JPL-Caltech / B. Williams (NCSU) (bc). **146-147 123RF.com:** picsfive (b). **147 123RF.com:** picsfive (t). **Eliot Herman:** (br).

NASA: ESA, CSA, STScI, T. Temim (Princeton University) (bc). **148-149 NASA:** ESA, J. DePasquale (STScI), and R. Hurt (Caltech / IPAC). **149 EHT Collaboration:** (br). **150 ESA:** Hubble & NASA (bl). **151 123RF.com:** picsfive (r). **Alamy Stock Photo:** Science Photo Library (cra). **ESA:** Hubble & NASA, S. Jha, L. Shatz (cr). **152-153 Dreamstime.com:** Mgallar. **153 ESO:** (br). **154 NASA and The Hubble Heritage Team (AURA/STScI):** A. Feild (STScI) (clb, crb). **NASA:** ESA, and The Hubble Heritage Team (STScI / AURA); J. Blakeslee (Washington State University) (br); JPL-Caltech / ESA / STScI / CXC (cb). **155 123RF.com:** picsfive (br). **Alamy Stock Photo:** Stocktrek Images, Inc. (cr). **Dreamstime.com:** Denys Bilytskyi (tl); Robyn Mackenzie / Robynmac (cb, tc). **NASA and The Hubble Heritage Team (AURA/STScI):** A. Feild (STScI) (cb/Irregular). **NASA:** JPL / Hubble (bl). **156-157 NASA. 157 NASA:** X-ray: NASA / CXC / SAO / J.DePasquale; IR: NASA / JPL-Caltech; Optical: NASA / STScI (br). **159 123RF.com:** picsfive (r). **NASA and The Hubble Heritage Team (AURA/STScI):** ESA, and the Hubble Heritage Team (STScI / AURA); (cra). **NASA:** H. Ford (JHU), G. Illingworth (UCSC / LO), M.Clampin (STScI), G. Hartig (STScI), the ACS Science Team, and ESA (tl); ESA, and the Hubble Heritage Team (STScI / AURA) (cr); JPL-Caltech / STScI-ESA (crb). **160-161 ESO. 161 Science Photo Library:** NASA / ESA / G. Bacon (STSCI) (br). **162 123RF.com:** picsfive (bl). **Dreamstime.com:** Robyn Mackenzie / Robynmac (clb, bc). **163 123RF.com:** picsfive (r). **NASA:** JPL-Caltech (crb). **164-165 NASA:** JPL. **165 Alamy Stock Photo:** Jrgen Flchle (crb). **166-167 Getty Images:** Stocktrek. **166 Dreamstime.com:** Robyn Mackenzie / Robynmac (cl). **NASA and The Hubble Heritage Team (AURA/STScI):** NASA, ESA, and Z. Levay (STScI) (clb). **167 Alamy Stock Photo:** NASA Image Collection (cr).

Cover images: Front: ESA: Davide De Martin & the ESO / NASA Photoshop FITS Liberator tr, NASA, ESA, CSA, B. Robertson (UC Santa Cruz), B. Johnson (Center for Astrophysics, Harvard & Smithsonian), S. Tacchella (University of Cambridge, M. Rieke (Univ. of Arizona), D. Eisenstein (Center for Astrophysics, Harvard & Smithsonian), A. Pagan (STScI) cl; **Getty Images / iStock:** Morgan Somers bl; **Lockheed Martin:** tr/ (GOES-R ART); **NASA:** ESA, and A. Simon (NASA Goddard) clb, JPL / DLR cla, cl/ (Callisto), cl/ (Ganymede), JPL / University of Arizona cla/ (Io); **Science Photo Library:** Dr Juerg Alean br, Carlos Clarivan bc, Miguel Claro tl; **Shutterstock.com:** buradaki c/ (Milky Way), Dmitriy Rybin c; Back: **ESA:** Davide De Martin & the ESO / NASA Photoshop FITS Liberator tl, NASA, ESA, CSA, B. Robertson (UC Santa Cruz), B. Johnson (Center for Astrophysics, Harvard & Smithsonian), S. Tacchella (University of Cambridge, M. Rieke (Univ. of Arizona), D. Eisenstein (Center for Astrophysics, Harvard & Smithsonian), A. Pagan (STScI) cr; **Getty Images / iStock:** Morgan Somers br; **Lockheed Martin:** tl/ (GOES-R ART); **NASA:** ESA, and A. Simon (NASA Goddard) crb, JPL / DLR cra, cr/ (Callisto), cr/ (Ganymede), JPL / University of Arizona cra/ (Io); **Science Photo Library:** Dr Juerg Alean bl, Carlos Clarivan bc, Miguel Claro tr; **Shutterstock.com:** buradaki c/ (Milky Way), Dmitriy Rybin c; Spine: **NASA and The Hubble Heritage Team (AURA/STScI):** NASA, ESA, J. DePasquale (STScI), and R. Hurt (Caltech / IPAC) cb; **NASA:** ESA, CSA, Brant Robertson (UC Santa Cruz), Ben Johnson (CfA), Sandro Tacchella (Cambridge), Marcia Rieke (University of Arizona), Daniel Eisenstein (CfA), with image processing by Alyssa Pagan (STScI) c; **Science Photo Library:** Carlos Clarivan t, Miguel Claro b.

All other images
© Dorling Kindersley Limited

About the authors

Sophie Allan is Head of Teaching and Learning at the National Space Academy, UK. She is passionate about space and has a wealth of experience delivering space education projects. Sophie has developed programs for the European Space Agency, Association of Science and Discovery Centres, and the Science and Technology Facilities Council. She has also delivered lectures on space science around the world and develops and teaches on the award-winning Space Engineering course taught in partnership with Loughborough College. Sophie has written and collaborated on multiple children's books with DK.

Josh Barker is Education and Outreach Officer for Space Park Leicester and the National Space Centre in the UK. For over a decade, he has shared his knowledge and passion for space and science with a range of audiences, from schoolchildren to science professionals. He has worked with science centers, planetariums, and space agencies, such as ESA. He has even taught space science on the Butlin's stage and at 10 Downing Street. Josh has also worked on a number of children's books with DK.

About the illustrator

Tim Smart has never been to space. If he were invited to be on the first spaceship to colonize Mars, he would probably go. Tim's favorite drawings in this book are the aurora fox and the Space Shuttle. He painted most of the work in this book in a small brick shed while listening to music and drinking black coffee.